"In today's pressurized workplaces, it's [ ] when it comes to leadership — knowing your strengths and how to use them, dealing with the things that may derail you, and becoming a great talent spotter so that you can lead through others. This book reminds us all about the most important leadership lessons and gives us a road map for putting them into action."

Michael Brooke, Head of Innovation, BNP Paribas Global Markets

"Discovering what your strengths are and building a work experience, and ultimately a career around them is one of the greatest opportunities afforded to readers of this book. Authors James Brook and Paul Brewerton have amassed a trove of ideas, insights and tools to guide the reader towards those areas of passion in their life, that will not only bring them greater personal satisfaction in their jobs, but also enable them to have greater impact at work, and ultimately in other areas of their life."

Stuart Crabb, Director of Learning, Facebook

"As a former Olympic medalist and current Olympic coach, I can't agree more with a strengths-based strategy. There is just so much more potential in people's strengths rather than fussing at the edges with their weaknesses. In addition, people are much happier working to their strengths and I know that happy athletes make better athletes. Paul and James' novel way of demonstrating the power of strengths and its four habits to build powerful leadership teams is captivating and like all good novels, very difficult to put down. I strongly recommend this book to all leaders and leaders to be."

Bill Barry, Managing Partner, Personal Best International Ltd

"Optimize Your Strengths is written as a fable, but it is based on reality. It describes the journey of a leader who moves from one worldview to another. Many people have had such epiphanies, but few have had the tools to move from enlightenment to execution to excellence. This book provides a practical toolkit for making that happen and achieving on-going success."

Mike Pegg, Author and Founder, The Strengths Foundation

"Brook and Brewerton offer four habits to stretch yourself beyond being an ordinary Joe at work. Optimize Your Strengths along with Joe on the path of possibility with shared vision, sparked engagement, skilled execution and sustained progress. Warning: This book may be habit forming and work may never be so limiting again."

David Zinger, Founder and Host of the 5000 member, Employee Engagement Network

"If you are serious about embarking on a journey to 'stretch' yourself and move forward professionally and personally, this book will be invaluable. James and Paul outline a positive and powerful approach to building on your strengths and addressing limitations. Through this enjoyable yet challenging story we're able to see the reality of just how transformational a change in thinking and behaviour can be. This is an important book which I would highly recommend to leaders and those aspiring to leadership."

Dr Rebecca Newton, Visiting Fellow, Department of Management, London School of Economics and Political Science

"A key question for those who want to help others is how to get new ideas across in a fun, interesting way which allows them to be painlessly absorbed. Brook and Brewerton achieve this by drawing on the inherent attraction of our brain to a good story. This book is immensely readable, packed with great information in an easy to digest style. I think managers, leaders and trainers alike will love this book, and I highly recommend it for those interested in developing their 'leadership edge.'"

Sarah Lewis, Psychologist, Author and Appreciative Inquiry Consultant

Optimize Your Strengths

Use your leadership strengths to get the best out of you and your team

James Brook and Dr Paul Brewerton

WILEY

Registered office

John Wiley and Sons Ltd, The Atrium, Southern Gate, Chichester, West Sussex, PO19 8SQ, United Kingdom

For details of our global editorial offices, for customer services and for information about how to apply for permission to reuse the copyright material in this book please see our website at www.wiley.com.

Library of Congress Cataloging-in-Publication Data

Names: Brook, James (HR consultant) author. | Brewerton, Paul, author.
Title: Optimize your strengths : use your leadership strengths to get the best out of you and your team / James Brook and Dr Paul Brewerton.
Description: Hoboken : Wiley, 2016.
Identifiers: LCCN 2015047538 | ISBN 9780857086938 (pbk.)
Subjects: LCSH: Leadership–Psychological aspects.
Classification: LCC HD57.7 .B756 2016 | DDC 658.4/092–dc23 LC record available at
 http://lccn.loc.gov/2015047538

A catalogue record for this book is available from the British Library.

ISBN 978-0-857-08693-8 (paperback) ISBN 978-0-857-08695-2 (ebk) ISBN 978-0-857-08696-9 (ebk)

Cover design: Wiley/Digital Parent Company

Set in 12/16pt Adobe Jenson Pro Regular by Aptara Inc., New Delhi, India

Printed in Great Britain by TJ International Ltd, Padstow, Cornwall, UK

Contents

Acknowledgements

This book has been over 18 months in the making and would not be finished without the contribution, inspiration and support of a large number of people.

Our deepest gratitude goes out to Nicki Hayes, who helped us transform this work from its rough early form to the polished story you are about to read. She demonstrated diligence and good humour throughout, exercising tremendous flexibility and talent in responding to our demanding expectations.

We also want to express special thanks to several other people who contributed to the book in a variety of ways: to Steph Tranter for her detailed and superb comments on virtually all aspects of the manuscript; to Gail MacIndoe for her early input into shaping some of the concepts and ideas in the book; to Sarah Glazier for her efficient support coordinating the production and marketing of the book; and to Dearbhla Kelly, Karena Gomez, Josh Dykstra, Aidan Tod, Mike Miller and Mike Pegg for their excellent comments and feedback during the final stages of writing.

Finally, a special note of thanks goes to our families for giving up time with us over the weekends, evenings and holidays, to help us complete this manuscript and for continuing to support us through every step of our journey to translate our dreams into reality. James wishes to thank his son, Liam, for remaining so positive over the years and bringing him so much joy and pride. Special thanks from Paul to Ana, his partner, and to his Mum for giving him all the strength and love in the world.

James and Paul, 2016

Foreword

There are many parallels between elite sport and business leadership, from which we can draw valuable inspiration to help navigate through today's increasingly turbulent and competitive business environment.

Just like top-performing athletes, effective business leaders have very different characters and strengths. They spend time analysing their strengths and natural abilities and find a place where they can shine. For business leaders, this also means using their strengths to free up and optimize the collective talents and abilities of team members in pursuit of a compelling vision.

However, the truly outstanding leaders don't stop there. Through hard work, dedication and continuous stretch – of themselves, others and the organization – they ensure they are always looking for ways to improve and take advantage of new opportunities. Like Olympic gold medalists, they don't rest on their laurels when they achieve success. They look to the next challenges and work hard to move beyond their comfort zone, inspiring others to do the same. Olympians know that, in their pursuit of gold, it is unlikely that they will be enjoying what they are doing all of the time. They engage in training routines that sometimes sap their energy and can't be delegated to others.

They must also learn to tackle their weaker areas through hard work and by drawing on their strengths and those of others, including their coach, colleagues and teammates. In business it is no different. Effective leaders remain mindful of their strengths to boost their confidence, resourcefulness and energy to overcome performance blockers. They tap into the talents of those around them, using their strengths to compensate for any areas of weakness.

I recommend this book because it is one of the few I have read that focuses on strengths building and provides practical guidance to help leaders discover their unique leadership edge, develop productive habits and achieve peak performance. Through understanding and practising the habits in this book, leaders can bring the best of themselves to their roles, inspiring passion, innovation and engagement in those they lead.

Kriss Akabusi, MBE, FPSA
Soldier, Olympic Athlete, Television Presenter
and Professional Speaker

Introduction

There are myriad different leadership models and approaches, many of which are highly prescriptive about the type of personality and qualities you need in order to be an effective leader. For example, qualities like charisma, persuasiveness, emotional intelligence and courage are often highlighted as essential qualities for leadership effectiveness and success.

However, recent research shows that successful leaders have very different personalities and qualities that they draw on in achieving their results. What they do have in common though is a true understanding of and ability to leverage their "leadership edge" (their unique strengths, abilities and skills) to influence and inspire others to achieve extraordinary results.

Effective leadership is also about positive stretch – stretching yourself and your team to push the boundaries and achieve in the upper range of your collective strengths. This is particularly relevant in today's competitive and evolving environment, where organizations (private, public and voluntary) are being challenged to do more with less, to work more efficiently by optimizing the discretionary effort, innovation and engagement of their workforce.

Our experience and research show that effective leaders master the art and science of "stretch". They adapt to environmental changes whilst adhering to the four Stretch Leadership™ Habits. They establish a clear "picture of success" for their own development and progression and that of their teams and the wider organization by *Sharing Vision* (the first Stretch Leadership™ Habit). They simplify this shared vision into manageable stretch goals ensuring buy-in from all stakeholders through the habit of *Sparking Engagement*. They *Skilfully Execute* (the third Stretch Leadership™ Habit) the road map to achieve their vision, celebrating success and *Sustaining Progress* (the final Stretch Leadership™ Habit) and positive energy throughout. In short, they push the boundaries of thinking and possibility, looking for new and innovative ways of doing things to achieve the organization's goals, while advancing their own career.

STYLE OF THE BOOK

This book is intended to be a practical and accessible work of fiction, rather than an academic text. It follows the journey of a leader with a deficit (or weakness-oriented) mindset gaining insight and experience about how to lead more effectively through stretching and optimizing his own strengths, as well as the strengths of his team, to achieve outstanding results.

The objective of this book is to highlight powerful concepts, principles and techniques of the strengths-based approach to achieving peak performance. We hope that our story brings these concepts to life in a relevant and engaging way. Whilst the narrative does not delve into the finer details of such models, we have included them as part of a resource and learning toolbox in the appendix of the book.

Although based on actual research and experiences from our own work and coaching, the characters and organization described in this book are fictional and do not reflect any specific person or organization. Whilst the story centres on a "for-profit" organization, the principles and concepts can be applied to any organization irrespective of the nature, purpose or size of the institution, as we have experienced over the past 20 years through extensive research and leadership development experience.

"*The leader's role is to free people, not control them – to free their strengths, ideas, energy and value, rather than straightjacketing them with bureaucracy.*"

Tony Hsieh, Managing Director, Zappos

Chapter 1

The Leadership Edge

In which Joe comes to terms with his predicament and challenges his beliefs about leadership...

J oe hangs up the phone on Kelly, his new boss, and walks slowly to his office window. Gazing thoughtfully across the park, he focuses on the wilting flowers in the hanging baskets, the product of a hot, dry summer. Wondering why the park wardens have not watered them, he smiles wryly, realizing that his estranged wife would say, if only she was there:

"You're only worrying about the park wardens, Joe, because it's easier than worrying about your own problems..."

In that second, he feels the full weight of his predicament for the first time.

As the recently appointed European head of Tiger Online Recruitment, Joe faces many challenges. His phone call with Kelly confirms this. His attention is momentarily drawn to a mother laughing as her two small children chase pigeons across the park. Frowning, he remembers his personal situation too, a situation he prefers not to think about.

"My life," thinks Joe, "is spinning out of control..."

Turning back to his desk, Joe forces himself to focus on his professional challenges. At the forefront of his mind is the firm's current financial performance. Sales are 25% behind target and several major accounts have not renewed their contracts in recent months. Kelly had called from Seattle, wanting to go through the numbers in detail to determine how to salvage the current year's performance. She had sounded even more agitated than usual, particularly since sales in the US and Asia Pacific had been hit badly by the sluggish economy too.

"What if these poor sales numbers are symptomatic of deeper, more malignant problems?" ponders Joe, as he looks out of the glass partitioning between his suite and the open plan office. Thinking about his leadership team, he counts all the ways in which their performance and behaviour fail to meet his expectations.

"Relationships between individuals are poor; there's a growing mistrust and some pretty unhealthy politicking taking place out there; Robert's resignation hasn't helped either," he assesses, clinically.

Robert, Tiger's former Finance Director, was Joe's top performer. He had applied for Joe's job. He didn't get it. He had moved to the position as CEO for Tiger's major competitor and Joe's former employer, Dragon Recruitment.

Spinning his chair towards the window, Joe stares out at the scorched landscape, wondering where to start. Suddenly he remembers meeting a guy on his return flight from Seattle two weeks ago. He was a "strengths coach". Joe had heard of business coaches, he'd even read a few books on business coaching; never though, had he heard of a strengths coach. Being curious by nature, Joe had spent some time getting to know this person, Richard, who had given him a business card when they parted at Heathrow. Joe recalls their conversation about the "deficit-based" belief system most people inherit from their childhood. Richard had explained that his job was to help leaders become more effective through focusing on strengths to achieve breakthrough thinking and to overcome challenges. At the time, Joe had been too embarrassed to admit that he was caught in the type of destructive habits Richard had described as typical of such a limiting belief system. Thinking about it now, he knew he'd had enough. He was tired of feeling trapped. It was time to find a way out and Richard's route had sounded kind of appealing.

Mulling over what Richard had shared with him on the plane, Joe gazes into the distance. Richard had been Chief Operating Officer for one of the UK's largest advertising firms before burnout forced him to take time out. An ambitious man, Richard had struggled to come to terms with his sudden and unexpected fall from the corporate ladder. Following six months away from work and a great deal of soul searching, Richard decided to become an executive coach. Sharing his learning, experiences and interpersonal strengths with others and helping them to succeed was the best choice he could take to move forward, he had said.

"I may end up burning out if I'm not careful. I think I'll call him," thinks Joe, as he reaches for his wallet to find Richard's business card.

A few seconds later, he has it. Picking up the phone, he makes the call…

*

The day before his meeting with Richard, Joe chairs his regular team meeting with Tiger's European Regional Executive Team (TERET).

The team comprises five members: Sally, the Sales and Marketing Director; Mark, the Operations Director; Raj, the Technical Director; Gwen, the Human Resources Director; and Phil, the new Finance Director (who is fast becoming Joe's right-hand man).

The meeting starts well, but within half an hour the usual petty in-house conflict kicks off. Mark and Raj had never seen eye-to-eye and this time their argument about a planned rebrand of the website is getting very personal.

"If you and your team can't get the site rebranded by January, we should go outside to a third party web design agency; at least they won't take holidays all the time, like you guys do!" Mark protests.

"Besides, rebranding our website should be a marketing project, not a technical project," adds Mark, looking hopefully at Sally, expecting her support.

"I'm getting frustrated with your constant criticism Mark," retorts Raj, irritably.

"You have no knowledge of web design, yet you are always criticizing what we're doing. We know what we are doing and want to do a proper job, not a half-baked one. That's why we're taking our time."

Exhausted, Joe ends the meeting, feeling utterly dejected. Yet again, his thoughts turn to his wife, Lynette. Lynette had recently left him. She had filed for divorce, citing his long work hours as one of the reasons. Joe had known that the relationship was becoming increasingly strained by his ambition and excessive working hours, but had never

ever imagined that Lynette would leave, taking their two young children, Harry and Amelia, with her.

*

Ten minutes into his meeting with Richard, Joe feels somewhat relieved. His fear of being subjected to psychoanalysis is receding. Richard appears to be more interested in what's going on in the business than in what's going on in Joe's head. Going into great detail to describe how the strengths coaching process works, Richard skilfully navigates Joe to a position of such comfort that, before Joe knows it, he is enjoying exploring in depth the strengths, weaknesses, opportunities and threats that Tiger faces.

"I am confident strengths coaching can help here, Joe. I sense you need quick results so I recommend we meet every two weeks over a six-month period, a coaching contract if you like. Let me explain a little more about what this would involve and what the outcomes will be," explains Richard.

"During these sessions, we will explore a proven approach that helps leaders stretch their strengths to achieve positive outcomes in terms of their purpose, their passion, their processes and their performance.

"We will start by getting a better understanding of what you bring to this leadership role and how you can combine your core strengths, values, aspirations and abilities to move beyond boundaries – perceived or real – and give yourself what we refer to as your leadership edge.[1]

---

[1] See Appendix, The Stretch Toolbox, 1.1. The Stretch Leadership™ Model.

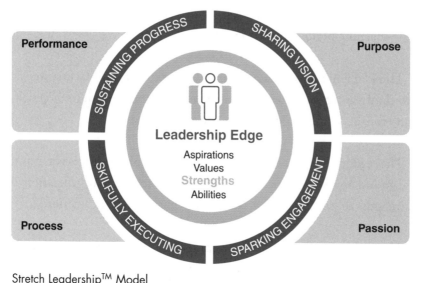

Stretch Leadership™ Model

"We will then explore the four habits of leaders at full strength: *Sharing Vision*; *Sparking Engagement*; *Skilfully Executing*; and *Sustaining Progress*. I say habits, because learning does not always translate into doing unless you choose to embed the learning with repeated behaviour, until that behaviour, that new way of being and doing, becomes automatic. Doing this, ultimately leads to better performance with very little need for external instruction or direction.

"We'll talk more about this; all you need to know for now is that, to help you adopt these habits, we'll look at some specific changes to your behaviour you may need to practise for a while until they become second nature.

"By the end of the final session, stretching your strengths – and those of your team – will have enabled you to lead your business to achieve the goals we agree on next week, and to sustain this success beyond the coaching period," he continues.

"Think of it like a continuous journey – an expedition. The first step is to clarify and clearly communicate your aspirations, both for yourself and for this organization (where you want to go).

"The second step is to ensure everyone is aware of where it is you want to go and how you can harness your personal, team and organizational strengths to get there (what you need to pack for the expedition).

"The third step is to take action, practising your learning (selecting the best route and starting out on the journey).

"The fourth step is to become agile in stretching (and sometimes contracting) your personal, team and organizational strengths across different situations (ensuring you adapt your route when conditions change to minimize risks and get to your destination in the best way possible).

"The fifth step is to recognize the successes and setbacks you have met along the path (comparable to taking time to enjoy and learn from your success when you get there, I guess).

"It's a five-step journey that allows you to grow gradually and sustainably. You move from aspirations to awareness, to action, to agility, to achievement.

"It is an ongoing journey though, Joe, because this naturally brings you right back to the beginning, reflecting and setting new aspirations for the next expedition."

Richard looks up at Joe, as if trying to gauge whether to continue. Seeing that Joe is open to more learning, Richard decides to push on. He reveals a slide on his screen.[2]

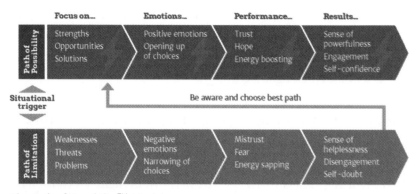

The Path of Possibility™ Model

"The question is, Joe, which route do you want to take? The path of limitation, where people feel stuck, isolated and full of self-doubt, with targets being missed? Or the path of possibility, leading to a sense of empowerment, where people find meaning in their work, and feel connected to the business's success and to each other, with targets routinely beaten?"

Joe silently reflects for a few seconds. For him, such a positive approach sounds a little too optimistic, especially considering the internal weaknesses and external threats he is facing.

"Thing is, Richard, I really don't know if I can. I'm not like you," he finally states.

"I mean, how do you do it? Or rather, how did you do it after you quit your job as COO of that advertising agency?"

---

2 See Appendix, The Stretch Toolbox, 1.2. The Path of Possibility™ Model.

"Ah. Well it is about conscious choice, Joe. I've trained myself and I act very deliberately to get back into a positive mindset when I feel myself slipping, as we all do from time to time. With strong self-awareness, self-discipline and lots of practice, you too can spend more time on this positive path. I'm not saying it will be easy. It will take a lot of conscious effort, but you can train your brain to walk this path. Anyone can," Richard replies looking directly at Joe.

"First you need the willingness to challenge and change your beliefs. Once you're aware of the beliefs that you hold that are limiting you, it takes conscious effort and deep practice to reprogram them. I started by recognizing things that triggered negative thoughts, feelings and actions and consciously tried to replace these with more productive ones. For example, after I first left the agency, when people asked what I was going to do next, I'd automatically change the subject because I didn't know the answer. I didn't know the answer because I still wanted to be winning those big advertising contracts. I still wanted to progress to CEO of the business and I couldn't see past what was not possible.

"I eventually realized that reacting in this way was draining, both physically and mentally. So, I chose to control the controllables and started practising to respond differently, at first with 'I'm not sure,' then with 'I want to help others,' and in the end with 'I'm going to be a coach.'"

"Your brain, Joe, is designed to be efficient. Everyone's is. So when your brain is under pressure, it will fall back into habits it learned early in life. Most of us have some unhealthy habits from childhood and other environmental factors. They place us on the path of limitation. We can only get off this path with a lot of self-awareness, hard work and deliberate practice," Richard is still looking directly at Joe.

"And I know what your next question is going to be, Joe," he smiles, his gaze losing its intensity.

"You do?" responds Joe, intrigued.

"Yup. You want to know if this is the right path for this organization and I can tell you that it was *made* for this organization. When you live in an unpredictable environment, you need to create a strong culture of learning, empowerment and personal accountability. It is the only way to remain agile. Normal management rules based on logical analysis and problem solving are not enough. Exploration, experimentation and collaborative working need to be encouraged. The path of possibility does just that.

Joe just looks at Richard as if he is an unfinished puzzle. Richard is familiar with this response and knows what to do next. He guides the conversation back to Joe's expectations of the coaching.

"So, where and how do you want to lead this organization, Joe? What would you like the outcomes of our coaching sessions to be?" he inquires.

Joe thinks they are obvious. "Improved results of course," he states bluntly.

"So, in order to achieve this, what areas of your current leadership style do you think we need to explore?" probes Richard.

Joe's thoughts turn immediately to his weaknesses. "Hmm, let me think. I suppose I don't, typically, involve other people enough in making decisions at work. I guess I'm fairly fixed in my views. I know what is best, I don't need persuading by others, so I just go about making it happen," he reflects.

"So, Joe, does that mean you tend to judge people really quickly and will close the book on them without trying to help them develop if your first impressions are not good?" Richard asks.

"I suppose so. I'm rarely open to persuasion and before the conversation we're having right now, it had never actually occurred to me to look for ways to help others develop and involve them in tough decisions!" admits Joe.

Richard listens attentively, making a few notes as Joe continues to talk about his weaknesses. Then, just as Joe begins to feel drained, Richard suggests, "Joe, why don't we spend some time reflecting on what you have achieved throughout your 15-year career?"

Joe is embarrassed "boasting" about what he has done well, especially in the light of all his problems. It just feels wrong. Richard smiles encouragingly. Before Joe realizes what is happening, he is recalling events and milestones in his career where he felt that he had triumphed.

"Winning the UK contract with that major oil company in my first role as a recruiter was a major turning point. It really accelerated my career. Getting headhunted by a large organization in the same industry and moving in-house as a general manager was massively rewarding too. It gave me real insights into the internal culture of large corporations.

"Then there are particular individuals that stick in my mind, where I found the perfect roles for their experience. I always get a big kick out of that. I'm still in touch with some of them: Diana, who successfully moved from a CFO to a CEO role, and Ahmed, who moved through the ranks to become Head of HR for a gas and oil company, to setting up his own recruitment business, spring to mind. There are quite a lot of people, now that I think about it.

"Getting this role was a high point too, believe it or not. At the time, it felt like winning a gold medal!" Joe reflects.

Richard decides that this is a good point to ask: "How does it feel talking about your successes, Joe?"

"I feel more energized than when we started. This morning I was beginning to lose hope. I felt trapped, looking over the edge. Now I can see that I have achieved a lot throughout my career," Joe admits.

Richard smiles warmly. Leaning towards Joe, he lowers his voice and asks, "What makes a business successful: focusing on fixing problems and weaknesses or focusing on company strengths and opportunities?"

Joe considers the question for 30 seconds. "Probably both," he replies.

"Exactly!" continues Richard, "and what percentage of your time and that of your team is focused on the company's problems, as opposed to its core capabilities and opportunities?"

"We definitely spend the majority of our time talking about issues and risks to the business," Joe admits without hesitation.

"So, let's imagine you switch this focus to spend 80% of your time and effort on your core strengths and opportunities as a leader and those of your team and the larger organization. The remaining 20% of your time can be focused on reducing weaker areas and other performance risks," Richard suggests.

"Really, it's all about ensuring the right balance, Joe. Research shows that if you spend the majority of your time and energy focusing on your strengths, knowledge and experience, optimizing your productive habits, and the remainder reducing performance risks, you will grow in terms of resilience, confidence and engagement, which in turn leads to achieving results," Richard explains with the help of a slide he swipes onto his screen.[3]

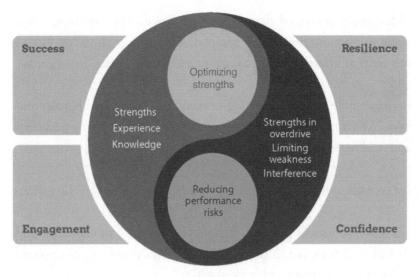

Positive Balance

"But we can't do that. We have too many problems at the moment!" protests Joe, rubbing the back of his neck and looking down at the

[3] See Appendix, The Stretch Toolbox, 1.3. Positive Balance.

notes he has been making. "And what do you mean by 'performance risks'? I remember you using this term on the plane as well," he adds.

"Performance risks are things that limit or get in the way of progress. There are three main types.

1. Limiting weaknesses – things that you're not good at and don't enjoy but which, if not done, may stop progress
2. Strengths in overdrive – things that you do enjoy and that you are good at but which, if overused or used in the wrong way or at the wrong time, can lead to negative outcomes
3. Other sources of interference – both those that come from yourself (such as being overly reliant on yourself or low self-confidence) and those that come from external sources (such as the company culture or the leadership style of its executives).

"Anyway, back to my original question, Joe: what if you were to spend 80% of your time and effort focusing on strengths and 20% focusing on reducing weaker areas and performance risks?" Richard asks.

He remains silent waiting for Joe to look up again. As Joe does, Richard meets his eyes and holds his gaze. Joe realizes that Richard is inviting him to reconsider what he has just said.

"Well, perhaps we can do both…I am starting to see that giving more attention to our strengths and opportunities might be really beneficial to get us off this precipice," contemplates Joe, rubbing the back of his neck again.

"Indeed," affirms Richard. "To get a team performing at the top of their game, it is important to focus on individual and collective strengths. Understanding and clearly communicating your own and your business's values, aspirations and abilities are vital too. The point where these four things meet is where you will find your leadership edge. The point at which the business's strengths, values, aspirations and abilities meet is where you'll find the key to this business's expansion too. We will explore this in detail at our next session."

"Woah! Slow down," interrupts Joe, leaning back in his chair, both hands behind his head. He is clearly irritated. "I am really concerned that we do not just ignore our weaknesses. And what about our failures? I know I've learned so much from mine. Surely reviewing failure – and lessons learned – is important? You seem to be navigating totally away from this. In fact, this is beginning to sound increasingly unrealistic. And like it's going to take forever," puffs Joe, rolling up his sleeves.

"My strengths, their strengths, values, aspirations and habits. Hell, Richard, I've not got time for all this. And what about experience and my team's ability to do the job? Isn't the experience and skills each one of them brings to the business just as important as this stuff? I've a business to run here you know, Richard. I haven't even got time to work out where to start!" Joe vents as he gets up from his chair and walks over to the window.

"Yes, Joe, I know. This *will* help you run your business. Just think about it for a minute. What will happen if you continue down the path you are currently on? You described to me earlier a culture of mistrust and pessimism. I can see that the culture here tends to focus on short-term wins rather than long-term successes. It is clear that your energy level, and their energy levels," Richard gestures towards the glass partition to the open plan office, "are not high. You've described to me all their – and your – shortcomings. You also said that talking about your successes and your strengths made you feel more 'energized'. That it made you feel less trapped, like there were more choices, right?" he asks.

"Right," replies Joe.

"Sure, people can learn a lot from failure and mistakes, but this is only half of the picture, Joe – they also learn a lot from doing new stuff, expanding their experience into areas where they are less comfortable. This is something that every leader needs to grasp to avoid getting stuck and limiting the potential of not just themselves but their team and, indeed, their organization."

"So, your first choice, Joe, is whether you want to get back into a more positive mindset, or stay in your current fixed mindset, keeping on a path that is inevitably going to limit you?"

"Before you answer, think about where your resistance is coming from. Is it just that you have got used to thinking in terms of failures and weaknesses, of fixing what's broken, rather than sharpening what's already great? Is it because you've been going down this path for so long that you've run out of steam and are unable to create choices? Where is this path going to lead you? And your team?" Richard concludes, pointing towards Joe's colleagues.

"As to where to start, I'm mailing you a link to an online strengths profiling tool, called Strengthscope360™. I'm sending you a user name and a password too so you can access the tool. If you take around 20 minutes to do this, we can prepare an in-depth strengths profile, which will help you understand your strengths as well as giving you feedback from your colleagues about how they view your strengths. The profile will help you to better understand your leadership style. It will suggest ways to up your contribution to this business by, for example, making the most of your strengths and your energy levels and practising the leadership habits we spoke about earlier.

"At our next session we'll review your profile, see what it tells us about you and look at how you can begin to share your vision of what this organization is capable of becoming. We'll also look at how to take the edge off any performance risks that may result from failing to manage any of those weaknesses you are concerned about. OK?"

"Sure," replies Joe half-heartedly, his mind already reflecting on the question Richard has just posed about where he'll end up if he stays on his current path. He knows he doesn't want to carry on as before but he is not yet convinced that he, or his organization, are ready to be stretched in these new ways.

"That's OK but I'm not happy signing up to a retainer contract with you yet. I want to see if this stuff works before committing. Can we come to a compromise, Richard?" he continues after a pause.

"What sort of a compromise, Joe?" asks an amused Richard.

"Well, can we trial this approach? Can I commit to, say, three meetings, and we review if it's working before committing to the six months?"

"Sure, Joe. We'll focus on identifying goals and getting some quick wins over the next six weeks. You'll soon see why this approach works," Richard reassures Joe. "One of the first positive patterns of behaviour to start purposefully practising is to complete a Learning Journal at the end of each session. Here's a journal. Just jot down the key things you learned today and find some time during the week to reflect on what you write," Richard concludes as he hands over a notebook to Joe, in which Joe is pleased to see copies of the models Richard introduced him to during the session.

"Yes, Sir!" jokes Joe.

"Great!" smiles Richard, closing up his laptop and getting ready to leave.

Having said goodbye to Richard, Joe returns to his office. He has a call scheduled with his solicitor to talk about divorce proceedings.

"Remembering my successes did feel good. I wish Lynette would remember what I did right as well as what I did wrong," he reflects as he accepts the call.

 Joe's Learning Journal entry

1. Maybe there's a different way to think about leading than the "fix it" attitude I've become used to. Focusing too much on given boundaries, weaknesses and failure may limit growth. A more positive mindset may help me to better engage stakeholders and get lasting success. I need to challenge my beliefs and weed out the unhealthy, self-limiting ones. I need to replace them with more positive, solutions-focused beliefs.
2. First, I need to understand more about my strengths and align these with my values, aspirations and abilities to find what makes me unique as a leader.

19

3. Then I need to change some of my behaviours to help me adopt the four habits Richard says are common to great leaders: sharing vision; sparking engagement; skilfully executing; and sustaining progress. This will lead to improved performance all round.
4. Staying positive will, hopefully, help me and the organization to succeed, but only time will tell.

Chapter 2

Habit 1: *Sharing Vision (stretch goals)*

In which Joe practises setting stretch goals...

Two weeks later, late one evening, Joe sits in his apartment assessing what he has learned from his first coaching session and the Strengthscope360™ profile, which he has just received.

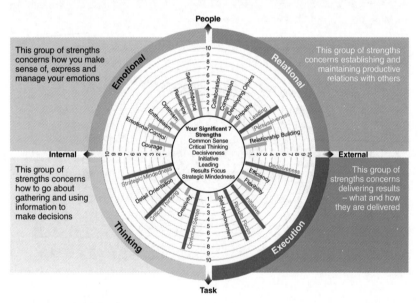

Joe's Strengths Wheel

According to his Strengthscope360™ feedback profile, his top strengths, described as his "Significant 7", are:

1. Critical Thinking
2. Decisiveness
3. Initiative
4. Leading
5. Results Focus
6. Common Sense
7. Strategic Mindedness.

Of these seven, several seem a bit vague; he will ask Richard about these at their next session, he decides. *Critical Thinking, Decisiveness, Leading* and *Results Focus*, however, speak to him loud and clear.

"Initiative?" he ponders. "Isn't initiative about ideas? I really wouldn't describe myself as an ideas person, but perhaps I'm going to need to be if I'm going to lead this team out of the mire we're in currently."

Reading further into his report, Joe learns a new definition of initiative: "taking independent action to make things happen and achieve goals".

"OK," he thinks, yes that fits. Reading on though, he notes an observation from a colleague (the online assessment had asked him to nominate up to eight colleagues to provide feedback on his strengths). Apparently, he sometimes takes the initiative too quickly, without seeking the opinions or approval of those his actions might affect.

He is pleased to see the *Results Focus* strength, which he recognizes immediately. Seeing the description of the "strength in overdrive" though (which the report defines as "a strength that can be overused to negative effect") is not so pleasing.

"Definition of Results Focus Strength in Overdrive: **in your drive for results, you may miss important aspects of task/project success, for example, the opportunity to reflect and learn, ensuring that people are engaged and recognized for their efforts," he reads.**

Strategic Mindedness is another strength Joe is relieved to see in his profile. Reading that his colleagues are not currently seeing this strength being used productively though comes as a bit of a shock.

In fact, focusing in further, he sees some patterns developing, "short-term focus" and "lack of direction" being the key themes. Joe stops reading the profile. He feels likes he's had the breath knocked out of him.

"I got the job for the exact strengths this profile highlights, so why aren't people seeing these strengths?" he ponders, trying to stop his thoughts racing.

He can't though. Reflecting on why his colleagues are not recognizing what he perceives as his strengths triggers more of Joe's own thoughts about the day's events:

"What will the implications be if I do actually think less about the problems we are facing and more about the strengths and opportunities?"

"How will this impact team morale, my relationship with Kelly and corporate HQ, and company performance?"

"Can any of these strengths help me out of my situation with Lynette?"

"Are the team going to think I'm a soft touch if I start babbling on about strengths, rather than targeting and removing our weaknesses, which are plain for everyone to see?"

"And, some of the team need a stick, not a carrot, to get them moving."

"And what if we find people aren't playing to their strengths and that their strengths don't fit? Who's going to do the actual real stuff that needs doing if we are going to make up the gap and hit our target?"

These questions, and more, cascade into Joe's consciousness late into the night, until his *Results Focus* strength kicks in and he begins to formulate a plan in his mind for the coming week.

"Successful people focus on making their strengths productive and don't dwell on their weaknesses," Richard had said. "They focus on what is possible, rather than on what it is that is limiting their success at this moment." This is a revolutionary idea to Joe. He has been brought up to believe that improvement is all about fixing bad points and weaknesses. This is certainly what he had been taught at school, at home and throughout his career. He even uses this approach in raising his own kids, focusing on their lower grades when their report cards arrive at the end of term, rather than the "A" grades, or at least encouraging a balance by looking at both. He is using it in his strategy for dealing with his broken marriage too.

Joe's thoughts spiral around his marriage and the children for a while, until he pulls back control, forcing himself to stop dwelling on his personal life and start addressing his professional one. Smiling to himself, Joe wonders what Kelly will make of all this strengths stuff. "Not much," he concludes.

Kelly is one of the toughest bosses Joe has ever worked for. She expects nothing short of excellence and keeps pushing for more, even in the face of tougher and tougher trading conditions. "She's just not going to get it," he thinks, without recognizing that the very thing he is annoyed with her about – her relentless pursuit for excellence – is one of his driving values, an integral part of who he is, driving how he behaves. In fact, his own relentless pursuit of excellence pretty much got him into the situation from which he is currently trying to escape.

Joe suddenly feels exhausted. Reflecting in this way does not come naturally to him. Switching off his computer, he goes to bed, hoping that he's tired enough to actually get a good night's sleep for a change.

The next morning, Joe is up and in the office even earlier than usual.

His first meeting is with Raj, who, no doubt, will complain about Mark's behaviour yesterday. Joe reflects on how to handle Raj and decides to take a new approach, inspired by what he had heard at yesterday's session. He chooses to suspend disbelief for the day.

As expected, Raj launches a barrage of complaints about Mark within the first few minutes of the meeting. Joe struggles to control his patience, but he listens carefully. When Raj finally finishes, he asks, "You and Mark have been working together for over two years now. Tell me about some of the successes you have shared."

Raj, clearly exasperated, states abruptly, "That's not the point. I think he needs to be pulled into line or I'll have to consider my future with Tiger."

Joe realizes this is going to be even harder than he had thought. "Just give this a try," he urges. "I want to understand your relationship better and how the current challenges have arisen."

"OK, but I really don't see how this is going to help," Raj says, reluctantly.

"Mark and I worked well together when I first started. We managed to launch the first website into the market in a record time of three months. We also launched the new agency module six months ago, which was a great success."

Encouraged by the noticeable softening in Raj's attitude, Joe pushes further. "What strengths did you guys use to achieve those results? By strengths I mean personal qualities that energize you and help you perform at your best," clarifies Joe.

"That's a tough question," responds Raj. "I suppose I am good at organizing and planning. I enjoy working out how to do things (and how not to do them) and I find it easy. Mark is not good at this. He just doesn't do details. He's really good with people though. It's clear he enjoys talking with our customers, and he's good at it. He gets all sorts of information from them that I would never be able to. He's a very creative thinker, whereas I'm more of a logical thinker, I guess."

Raj falls silent for a while, reflecting on what he has just said. "Come to think of it, we do have strengths and skills that complement each other, but we can't seem to communicate with each other anymore, even at a basic level. These days, working with him just exhausts me."

Joe realizes he will have to dig deep to help Raj and Mark find a way forward. If he doesn't, he'll be risking losing one (or both) of them from the business. With Robert's recent departure, this wouldn't be a good outcome.

"OK," Joe says, standing up and walking to join Raj on the other side of the desk. "I have an idea that might get your relationship back on track. Do you want to hear it?"

"Why not?" asks Raj, not sounding terribly committed, though secretly intrigued by what his boss is about to say. "We've tried everything else recently. Even Gwen in HR had a go at helping us, so you may as well throw your ideas into the ring," he adds.

Joe decides to go for it.

"I'd like you and Mark to think about your successes over the past two years and the strengths and skills you used when your relationship was, shall we say, more 'productive'. I'd also like you to think about how you can use these strong points, and your past achievements, perhaps borrowing from each other's strengths to get your relationship back on track. I suggest you both take a couple of days to do this and each write down key points and insights to bring along to a meeting with me. We can then discuss how you get past your current difficulties and move forward, using the website rebrand as a project. I will try to get Mark's commitment to do this too and I will let you know the minute I know his thoughts."

Raj looks at Joe, bemused, and says, "OK, I'm willing to give it a try, but I warn you, I'm not holding out much hope."

Joe thanks Raj and, after Raj has left the office, returns to his chair wondering if he has done the right thing.

"I know exactly what's the matter with those two. They just wind each other up and always will. One of them needs to go. Why am I playing around with this strengths stuff? If I get them to do it, I'll have to get the others to do it too. It will be anarchy with everyone running around trying to identify their strengths and nobody focusing on hitting our targets.

"Still, '*if you always do what you've always done, you always get what you always got*,' as Lynette says. At least this is a different approach," he thinks. "What's the worst that can happen?"

Little does Joe know that he has just, in Richard's language, "stretched" his *Decisiveness, Initiative* and *Critical Thinking* strengths, combining them in a new way and pushing himself beyond his comfort zone. He has also tasked Raj and Mark with a stretch project.

"So, Joe, how was your week?" asks Richard as he enters Joe's office.

"Well, I could say, 'It's been emotional', but as you will see from my Strengthscope360^{TM} profile, I'm not exactly an emotional person. So, let's just say it's been 'thought provoking' shall we?" states Joe in a tone that implies humor yet clearly masks anxiety.

"Ah, so you spotted that most of your standout strengths lie in the bottom two clusters of the 'strengths wheel', meaning that you are more task-focused than people-focused?" asks Richard.

"Yes. And of course I am more task-focused than people-focused at work. I'm meant to be a leader and leaders focus on tasks and results. I employ other people, like Gwen, to do the people stuff," Joe replies, a little confrontationally.

"I allow people to see my feelings more in my personal life though," he continues, his tone softening as he suddenly realizes that his personal life is fast becoming non-existent.

"So there are two 'Joes' here are there? The professional Joe and the at home Joe?" Richard prompts.

"I suppose so," replies Joe.

"Or is it that there is only one you but you have just learned to express yourself differently in different situations because of what you think is valued in each context?"

Joe just looks at Richard. He makes no response. Richard, aware that Joe is processing a lot of information and suppressed emotion, continues:

"Great teams are made up of people with emotional, relational, thinking and execution strengths."

"Nobody can be strong in all four areas. There is no such thing as a well-rounded leader. Every leader has areas of strength and areas of limitation. Great leaders recognize what they do and don't have and call on the strengths of those around them to make up for their limitations. Being strong is not about having to do everything yourself. Strong people and strong teams know how to borrow strengths from, and lend strengths to, other people. In the natural world this is called interdependence. There is a lot we can learn from the natural world. Setting up successful businesses is not dissimilar to setting up successful ecosystems. At the end of the day, everything needs homeostasis – or balance – to thrive.

"Think of a soccer team. You wouldn't play your best striker in goal would you? Soccer teams collectively cover each position on the pitch. The best teams have each player in a position that plays to their strengths. The best business teams collectively cover each area of the strengths wheel, with each team member in a role that plays to their strengths. Get this right and you've everything you need to move beyond any boundary or obstacle, real or perceived. You will be able to move in whichever direction you set," adds Richard, neatly bringing the conversation round to the subject of setting stretch goals – an important behavioural pattern associated with the first Stretch Leadership™ Habit, *Sharing Vision*, and the planned topic for the session.

"And to ensure you achieve even the most challenging goals," he adds purposefully.

Joe absorbs the words on the strengths wheel Richard is showing him. Knowing that he scores highly in thinking and execution strengths and less so in emotional and relational strengths is feeling less threatening. "In fact," he considers, "It's comforting to think that members of my leadership team may have some of the strengths I lack."

"So, I said last week that we'd review your strengths profile before trying to find your leadership edge and learning about the first Stretch Leadership™ Habit – *Sharing Vision*. Let's take a look at it. Did you recognize yourself? Have you noticed yourself using any of these strengths this week?"

Joe goes on to describe his thoughts about the strengths he recognizes and the ones he doesn't. Typically, Joe starts by focusing on what he does not recognize, what he does not like or agree with. Richard skilfully guides him towards recognizing and celebrating the strengths that he has and the power he has to dial them up and down, according to the needs of specific situations.

"It's kind of like turning the volume up and down on a radio. You can have it on as loud as you like when you're alone and not trying to focus on anything else. When you're in a public place, such as on a train or in a park though, it's always wise to exercise caution and think about your impact on others."

Feeling encouraged, Joe tells Richard about his new approach with Raj and Mark. Richard immediately picks up on this.

"Ah, well there you go, you say you do not see *Initiative* as a strength, yet did you not use your *Initiative* in finding a new way to look at the issues caused by Raj and Mark's working relationship?"

"Well, I guess that's one way of looking at it," Joe says thoughtfully.

"In fact you did more than exercise your *Initiative* strength. You combined it with two of your top strengths, the strengths that really describe who you are, *Decisiveness* and *Critical Thinking*, in a totally new way. That is what we call 'stretch'. You stretch your strengths by using them in a new way, outside of your comfort zone. It's one way to overcome obstacles or barriers, Joe, and you're already doing it intuitively. Not only are you stretching yourself, Joe, you have also set two members of your leadership team a stretch project. This is positive Joe, and can really make a difference when seen as part of building a strengths-based culture" Richard enthuses.

Joe smiles. Things had actually been going quite well with the Raj/Mark situation and Joe was already seeing some benefits to his new approach.

"We'll talk more about this later and about how to optimize your strengths, and those of your colleagues, as well as how to deal with any performance risks these strengths in overdrive (or any lack of strengths) may cause. First though, let's investigate your 'leadership brand': who you are; what you bring to this organization; what difference you want to make here; and how you want people to view you as a leader," says Richard, pulling up a slide on his screen that looked similar to the type of brand pyramid Joe was more familiar with as a marketing communications tool.[1]

"We're going to work our way up your personal pyramid, Joe. It's a great way to help you understand, or crystallize, what it is that makes you leadership material and why people trust and respect you, why they listen to you.

"It begins with understanding your core values: you know, the type of inbuilt attitudes you have that guide what you do. What do you think these are?" Richard asks.

---

[1] See Appendix, The Stretch Toolbox, 1.4 Leadership Brand Pyramid.

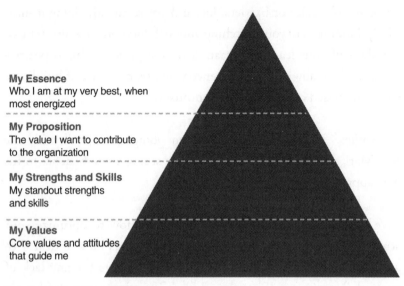

My Essence
Who I am at my very best, when
most energized

My Proposition
The value I want to contribute
to the organization

My Strengths and Skills
My standout strengths
and skills

My Values
Core values and attitudes
that guide me

The Leadership Brand Pyramid

"I'm not sure how to describe my values, I know that I always want people to be up front and honest with me. I can't stand it when people don't tell you the truth and you don't know what you are dealing with," contemplates Joe.

"So, do you think one of your values is 'truth'?" suggests Richard.

"I don't know. That doesn't quite fit. I just want people to own up and be honest if a mistake is made," Joe responds.

"Perhaps it's 'honesty' then?" clarifies Richard.

"Yes, that seems more like what I'm describing," agrees Joe.

"OK, so what else, what is really important to you about the way you work with people and how they work with you?" pushes Richard.

"Well, I can't stand people who aren't focused, who seem to daw-dle when there is no need. I like people to care and have a sense of urgency – we need to react and act quickly. There are times to be thoughtful but I get really irritated when people just don't get on with things," Joe explains.

"So is it about being 'focused' – that was a word you just used?"

"It's more than that, it's about going at speed, picking up the pace," Joe is living his value without realizing it. Before Richard has a chance to make another suggestion, Joe exclaims:

"That's it, 'pace'. I want us all to have pace, not feel rushed but just to work at pace.

"But I also value people with integrity, hard workers and those who take on a team-oriented work ethic. I value passion, commitment; I could think of lots more words. It's really hard to identify just a few!"

"Yes I understand that. How about we decide on a few now and you take the list away and do a bit more thinking on it. The best way to get clarity is to rank your values in order of importance. Remember that values are your internal compass. They guide the way you behave. So if you're struggling to order them, think about a real and difficult situation you are in and ask yourself, 'which of these values would I use navigate my way through?' Try to distil down to three or four values, like four points on a compass," Richard summarizes.

Working through his Significant 7 strengths, as identified in his strengths profile, Joe identifies his top strengths as *Critical Thinking* and *Results Focus*. He adds "market knowledge" and "broad business experience" as the specific skills and expertise he brings to the organization.

Moving up to the next level though, Joe begins to struggle.

"I'm not sure I understand the difference between my proposition and my essence, aren't they saying the same thing?" Joe asks.

"You're right, they are, but what's different is who they are targeted at. The proposition is mainly for you. It is your way of describing the difference you wish to make; the value you intend to bring. The essence is for other people. It reflects how you want your leadership value to be described by others in 5–10 seconds," Richard clarifies.

"Oh right. How should I go about deciding on what my proposition is, there are so many things I'd like to achieve?" Joe responds.

"Well, it's the one thing you want to be remembered for. What do you care most about? If there was one thing people remembered you for, what would it be?" guides Richard.

"Wow that's a hard one. That's like blowing my own trumpet, and I'm not sure I'm comfortable with that. Who am I to say that I will be memorable and what happens if people don't remember me for what I want to be remembered for?" Joe stalls.

"That's a very normal and natural reaction to the question, Joe. Try looking at it another way: if you don't know where you are going, how will you know when you have got there? If you don't define a goal, how will you know what to focus your energy on? One of your strengths is

Results Focus isn't it? This is all about applying that strength to defining and achieving your personal brand. How do you apply your *Results Focus* strength to work tasks?" Richard pushes.

Joe looks thoughtful and does not speak for at least a minute. The silence is noticeable but comfortable.

"I guess you're right. At work, I clearly define what we want to achieve with the team and then I go all out to damn well make sure we achieve it," is his eventual response.

"So could you apply that here? How do you decide what to focus on at work? There must be lots of things that need to be done, how do you decide which goals to set?" Richard prompts.

"Well, the most important and pressing," replies Joe, as if he thinks the answer is obvious.

"So what's the most important and pressing thing that you want to do as a leader?" persists Richard.

"Well, it's about people I think. It's about getting people to work together and achieve more than they initially thought possible," Joe summarizes.

"So, how do you want to be remembered, Joe?" asks Richard, smiling inwardly as he remembers Joe's earlier comment about employing other people to do "the people stuff".

"As someone who delivered and who made teams work to produce exceptional results," concludes Joe.

"So that's your proposition Joe. And how can you express this as a motto, a motivational call to action that will engage your team to do their best for you? What is your essence?"

"Something like...*delivering the best, together* perhaps," Joe responds.

Reviewing the completed pyramid on his screen, Richard is curious about the legacy Joe wishes to leave at Tiger. With further prompting about what a good team looks like, Joe describes a thriving business where people show up at work wanting to do their very best, enjoy what they do and always meet their targets.

"So you want to create a thriving business where people bring the best of themselves to work, enjoy what they do and always hit their targets, right?" asks Richard.

"Yup," nods Joe.

"So, for someone who is task focused, I am interested in why you think it is important for people to enjoy their work?" Richard probes, delighted at the speed with which Joe seems to be navigating towards the path of possibility.

"Because if people enjoy what they do, it's not a struggle. They feel upbeat and energized and this positive energy becomes the norm, the way things are done. With an environment where there is positive energy, things get done. Targets get met. It's as simple as that," responds Joe, surprised at how enthusiastic he is feeling.

"I guess it's what you call taking the path of possibility," he adds thoughtfully. "I want to lead people towards this path. I've had enough of uphill battles and getting stuck in a swamp of problems and poor morale. It's about time we stopped being victims here and show ourselves to be capable of growth."

"Good. You are already thinking like the leader of a top team. You have a good understanding of who you are as a leader and hopefully this pyramid will help you to communicate that to your team. Once they know what you expect of them – and what they should expect from you – your role as a leader will become easier. It will become easier still if you take a close look at your team's strengths profiles to ensure that you have everything you need to realize your vision.

"Then all you need to do is to share your vision by creating a rallying call that will inspire and motivate your team to want to join the journey. We'll talk about this later, how to express a vision, or a mission, in a way that will take people along with you. First though, you need to focus on the end result, where it is you want to take your team. So, let's have a look at how to set stretch goals.

"What do you think a stretch goal is, Joe?" Richard asks.

"A goal that challenges you to push yourself beyond where you are," suggests Joe, thinking as he says this that all goals are designed to do that, making the word "stretch" kind of redundant.

"Yes. It's even more. It's a goal that positively challenges you to move beyond your comfort zone by stretching your strengths and expertise to achieve a new, clearly identified level. Successful organizations build this approach into their performance management and staff development systems as part of the journey towards building a strengths-based culture. This helps employees stretch their performance to new levels.

Richard picks up an elastic band. He holds up his left hand, the band loosely draped over his thumb and index finger. Moving his finger and thumb apart, he stretches the band so that the edges are straight but not tight. Simultaneously he swipes an image onto his screen.[2]

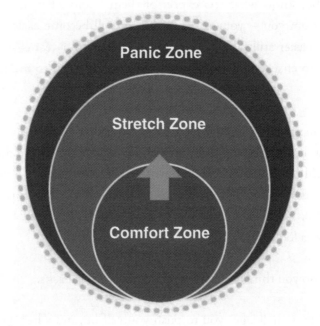

The Stretch Zone

"Stretch goals take you from here, your comfort zone, to here," he moves his fingers apart stretching the band further, "the point of stretch," with his other hand, he hovers his cursor above the arrow in the image on his screen, "to here," his fingers are as far apart as they

---

[2] See Appendix, The Stretch Toolbox, 1.5. The Stretch Zone.

can get – almost – the band stretching to its limits, "the stretch zone, where you are performing at your best."

"The art of setting stretch goals is to take yourself, your team and your organization to here, but not to," Richard stretches his finger and thumb that extra few millimetres apart and the band snaps "here – the panic zone," he concludes.

"The way to do this is to practise the four Stretch Leadership™ Habits. OK?" checks Richard.

"OK," replies Joe, looking down at the broken band. He has never empathized with an item of stationery before.

"Good. Now, you are already setting stretch goals for your team – that project you gave to Raj and Mark is a sort of stretch project. If you had formally set it up as a development project for them, how would you have described it?"

"To combine their strengths in a way that compensated for their weaknesses in order to deliver the rebrand of the website on time and within budget?" suggests Joe.

"Good, but when communicating goals, or a corporate vision come to that, try starting at the end – the outcome you want. That's where all top performers start in all walks of life – by clearly identifying their goal – the trophy they wish to lift. They then work backwards to where they are now in order to work out how to get there. Try being specific about the details too, the timings and the costs here, for example," Richard advises.

"So, 'to deliver a rebranded website by the end of the quarter for under £20,000, combining the team's individual strengths, skills and expertise' perhaps?" clarifies Joe, picking up on the language used in his strengths profile, and by Richard.

"Excellent," encourages Richard. "The key is to set people goals that challenge their performance to reach peak capacity. This is not about 'cracking the whip' and working people harder to meet short-term results, which can actually be demotivating and demoralizing. It's about setting an ambitious vision for the organization that people can relate to and breaking work down into manageable phases, or goals, that people find inspiring and morale boosting."

"Have you heard about the Eliza Doolittle Principle?" continues Richard.

Joe ponders the question for a moment before answering "Is that from *My Fair Lady*, when the pompous British linguist gives speech lessons to a flower girl to try and turn her into a lady? I remember seeing the stage show in London years ago."

"That's the one," replies Richard. "The underlying principle is the important thing I want to stress here: people will perform to the level of expectation that is created for them. This is an incredibly powerful effect that has been proven through several decades of research. So, if leaders have positive, stretching expectations of their staff, they will generally live up to these, and even over-deliver. This is illustrated in *My Fair Lady* as Eliza Doolittle starts to become a lady when Professor Higgins attitude and behaviour towards her shifts and reflects the belief that she can, despite all odds, become a lady reflecting elite

London society. Conversely, if you have negative expectations of people, they are likely to perform *down* to these negative expectations."

"I think I get it. So, if we set challenging and realistic – but stretching – goals for people and reinforce through our words and actions that we expect them to achieve these, they will generally meet or surpass those goals," reflects Joe.

"Absolutely," responds Richard. "One of the crucial roles of any leader is to set the expectation that everyone can, and should, become better and better."

"So how about a stretch project for you, Joe? What might your goal be, taking into account that legacy we've been talking about? Let's start there – at the end – how you want to be remembered," Richard pushes on.

Twenty minutes later and Joe feels invigorated. Working from the end to the beginning intrigues him. It reminds him of how he had worked out his training schedule when he'd run a marathon ten years earlier, before he'd had children. It reminds him of a speech he'd once heard the basketball player Michael Jordan give about successful rituals and routines. It gives him an idea about how to create some happy memories for his children too – a family stretch project. Joe is in his element.

"How are you feeling, Joe?" asks Richard, as Joe purposefully adds a full stop to the final leadership goal he has just identified for himself:

Long-term goal: Within the next three years, to create a business with key talent retention rates of 90%, employee satisfaction rates of 85%, where revenue has increased by 150% and profit has increased by 40%, through aligning individuals' strengths to their roles and creating a culture where individuals combine their strengths to get the job done.

Medium-term goal: By the end of the year, to align the job roles of my leadership team to their strengths, according to the outcomes of their stretch projects, in a way that will continue the drive towards a 50% revenue growth target by year end.

Short-term goal: By the end of the quarter, to profile the strengths of my leadership team and set each of them a goal that will drive towards a 25% revenue growth target by end quarter.

"Good," Joe replies. "Like I need to start clarifying all this and communicating it with the rest of the leadership team, drawing on their strengths for support and guidance, of course."

"Great! And communicating 'all this' is about more than writing the sort of mission and vision statement you can pull a template down from Google for. It's about developing a vision together, as a team, describing what it's actually going to look and feel like when you – collectively – reach your goals. But, again, we are jumping ahead!" Richard concludes, pleased that Joe seems to be getting it so quickly.

"So, Joe, you may not realize it yet, but you're finding your way along this pathway intuitively. You've already picked up yourself that your *Decisiveness* strength may lead to you making decisions based on short-term outcomes, for example. This is something we'll work on next week, when we'll learn about the second behavioural pattern that will embed the *Sharing Vision* habit: optimizing strengths."

Returning to his office after saying goodbye to Richard, Joe is struck by Richard's earlier comment about being strong is not the same as being self-sufficient. It echoes one of Lynette's mantras:

"Marriage is meant to be a partnership, Joe. I'm fed up of making these decisions alone then being criticized for getting it wrong. If you want to be in control, try turning up sometimes. Either that or go! It would actually be easier to be a single parent."

Joe picks up the phone to Lynette. He thinks it is probably a good idea to get her feedback and buy-in to the project he has in mind for the kids, and now he has it in mind, he doesn't want to waste any time.

 Joe's Learning Journal entry

1. I've clarified my leadership brand and started to understand how I can contribute value as a leader. It feels like our organizational values are similar to my personal values, so I do belong here. I think my personal values are aligned with Kelly's values. Maybe I find her so frustrating because she reminds me that I am not living my values?

2. I do actually believe that I can use my personal strengths, and our collective strengths, to get us out of the mess we are in. I am going to need to chunk it up though into short-, medium- and long-term goals, and not allow the big picture to

be threatened by short-term thinking. People think that I act too quickly without bringing in others early enough sometimes. This may be because my *Decisiveness* strength can lead me away from the long-term goal and cause me to act independently.

3. My top strengths are: *Results Focus, Critical Thinking* and *Decisiveness.* I may need to dial some of these down sometimes, such as my *Decisiveness* strength. I may also need to combine these with some of my colleagues' top strengths sometimes to overcome some of my weaknesses. They can borrow from my strengths store too, to overcome theirs. We just need to understand more about each other's strengths and the dynamics to do this.

4. I need to build support for a shared vision by clarifying and communicating all of this in a way that describes what it's going to look and feel like when we reach our goals, remembering to bring the team in so that we develop the plan together.

5. All of the above relates to setting stretch goals – an important part of *Sharing Vision.* This is the first Stretch Leadership™ Habit. If I deliberately and diligently practise setting stretching goals, sharing vision will soon become second nature.

Chapter 3

Habit 1: *Sharing Vision (optimizing strengths)*

In which Joe practises optimizing his strengths...

Joe's meeting with Richard is to start 15 minutes late. He is stuck on a call with Kelly, who is criticizing the previous month's sales, which are 8% down on the month before. Kelly is clearly not satisfied with his explanation and has little sympathy for the staff problems he is experiencing. She is about to drop a bombshell...

"We gave you this job because we felt you had the leadership ability to deal with these issues, Joe, so don't bring me complaints about your team. You know you have the authority to hire and fire team members, so, if they're not working out, find people who have the right skills and attitude to get the job done. There is only one proviso, and this is something you are going to have to share with the rest of your staff: we're having to cut budgets across the business, so you cannot make any pay increases, or pay any commission-related bonuses, even if a member of your team meets their individual target. We're all in this together, Joe. Got it?" queries Kelly.

"Got it," replies Joe, after a short pause, uncharacteristically struggling to find words.

Kelly's harsh words still ringing in his ear, Joe sits down for his two-hour meeting with Richard.

"You don't look terribly happy, Joe," observes Richard.

"No. My head is spinning. I've just had another bawling out from my boss, Kelly. She doesn't appreciate the problems I have here in Europe. This is a different market than the US. She just doesn't get the cultural differences. She expects me to tell my team that there is a pay freeze and no commission will be paid, even if they meet their targets! This is a commission-based business. How on earth she expects me to motivate them without the money incentive I really do not know," Joe vents.

Richard had planned to start by reviewing Joe's progress against the goals he had set himself in the previous session. However, given the mood Joe is in and the conversation he has just had with Kelly, Richard decides to change tack and help Joe understand how he can optimize his strengths to move himself back towards the path of possibility.

"OK, Joe, the good news is that there are plenty of ways to motivate people, other than with money. Research shows that motivation stemming from within ... in other words, making work more interesting by tailoring jobs to fit people's strengths, beliefs and values, or recruiting people for their strengths, beliefs and values, is more sustainable.

"The key is getting your team to share and believe in a vision and ensure that they are provided with opportunities to apply and stretch their strengths in a way that contributes to this vision. This is a vital part of the first Stretch Leadership^{TM} Habit, which is what today's session is going to focus on. OK?"

"OK," sighs a subdued Joe.

"Optimizing strengths – those of your team as well as your own – is a key behaviour you need to build into your routine if you are going to embed all the leadership habits, but especially the first habit, *Sharing Vision*. Effective leadership is about stretching yourself, your team and the organization. Optimizing strengths is the starting point.

"Now is the perfect time to start optimizing strengths, Joe. You're already practising this subconsciously to some extent. By the end of this session you'll understand exactly what you can do to get these guys motivated, regardless of the bad news about the pay freeze. Ready?"

"Go on," prompts Joe, genuinely keen to hear what Richard will say next, but struggling to concentrate on the words coming out of Richard's mouth as what he's just heard from Kelly is still echoing in his head.

"Remember the conversation we had in our first session about this coaching process taking you from aspirations to awareness, to action, to agility to achievement and then to revisit your aspirations? Let's try to use your current situation with Kelly to move from awareness to action. Ready?" asks Richard.

"OK," Joe mutters, slipping back into reluctant mode whilst rolling up his sleeves.

"So what do you value about Kelly as a boss, Joe? What are her strengths?" invites Richard.

Joe's face drops. He is still angry about the conversation with Kelly and doesn't really want to acknowlege anything positive about her right now. Still, he pulls himself round quickly enough, lifting his head and answering: "Well, Kelly's one of the smartest people I know. She totally understands the online recruitment business and gives me a lot of latitude to do what I want. She will not accept excuses or second bests, so I guess she shares some of my strengths – like maybe *Leading*, *Results Focus* and *Strategic Mindedness*."

"Taking into account what you have just said about her strengths, and what you now know about your own strengths, what style is going to work best with her, what do you need to do to play to your collective strengths?" inquires Richard.

"I suppose I need to take more accountability. I need to take solutions to Kelly, rather than problems. I also need to ensure I know my stuff and am well prepared for our conversations. However, I always feel she's not the most approachable person; it's weird but I am unusually anxious when she's around. I would love to tap into her competitor and industry knowledge, but feel I can't ask her for help with this."

Richard smiles, aware that Joe is already moving away from his pattern of self-reliance, in his mind at least. Since reinventing himself as a strengths coach he has seen many successes. Even so, he still enjoys the rush of excitement he feels every time he senses these familiar turning points.

"Why is that, Joe? Why do you feel you can't ask Kelly for help?" he prompts.

Joe looks at the floor, as if he keeps a store cupboard of answers there. After a long pause, he replies:

"I don't want her to know what I don't know. I feel it makes me look weak."

"OK, let's be practical about this. *Common Sense* is one of your strengths; let's use it to see if we can move ourselves onto that upper path I showed you in our first session – the path of possibility – remember?" Richard stops to clarify.

"Yes, the path that those with growth mindsets take, where you get feelings of self-esteem and personal achievement. I remember," replies Joe a little sarcastically.

"Based on what you have told me about Kelly, you share some strengths, and certainly share some values, so can you try to empathize with her for a moment? If one of your team came to you and asked for advice or help, how would you feel?"

"I'd be pleased they'd shown initiative and I'd jump at the chance to share my knowledge. Being *Results Focused* and *Strategically Minded*, I love any opportunity to help fix things," responds Joe, bringing his gaze up to table level.

"And which strengths did you say you shared with Kelly?"

"Probably *Leading, Results Focus* and *Strategic Mindedness,*" responds Joe, meeting Richard's eyes.

"So how do you think she'd respond to being asked for help?"

"She'd love it at the time. But after helping, she may judge me for not knowing my stuff in the first place," Joe responds, his *Critical Thinking* strength entering overdrive.

"Would you judge a member of your team in this situation?" asks Richard.

"Only if they hadn't thought it through properly in the first place, had come to me with something non-specific or which added no value to the outcomes we're driving towards."

"So, what are you going to do about approaching Kelly and tapping into her industry knowledge?" Richard pushes.

"I'm going to work out, exactly, what it is I want to learn from her and why, then go to her with specific, well thought out, questions."

"So how do you feel about Kelly now and asking her for help?" prompts Richard.

"Well, I can see how my assumptions about how she would react are just that, assumptions. In fact she may react how I would react. I think I just need to put a bit of thought into it before I approach her, which is fair enough," Joe replies.

"That all sounds good, and how do you feel?"

"More able to deal with it actually, not so afraid or anxious about it. Well, maybe still a bit afraid," says Joe with a wry smile, "but definitely more confident to do it."

"Good. Perhaps this is a good time to talk about how to ensure you are managing the potential consequences of any performance risks this team's individual and shared strengths may present. Can you remember what the three types of performance risk are? We talked about them at our last session," Richard asks, wondering if Joe will recognize that he has just come very close to allowing his *Critical Thinking* strength to go into overdrive and hijack his *Initiative* strength. Richard pulls up Joe's Strengthscope360™ profile to help along their discussion.

"Yes 'limiting weaknesses', strengths in 'overdrive' and both internal and external 'sources of interference'," Joe responds, not in the mood to go into detail as he wants to move forward, not reflect on last week's learning.

Realizing that Joe may be able to repeat learning parrot fashion, but was not necessarily yet absorbing the learning and putting it into practice, Richard decides to persevere.

"To be effective, strengths need to be matched to the requirements of the situation. Leaders need to watch out for unintended consequences associated with strengths, which can easily arise. Let's look at the first performance risk, 'limiting weaknesses'. Do you think you have any limiting weaknesses, Joe?" probes Richard.

"Well yes. I am not creative, developing others does not come naturally to me – so not being able to offer pay-related rewards kind of leaves me feeling toothless, and, before you point it out to me, yes I know, optimism is not one of my strengths," Joe responds, a little defensively.

Richard realizes that he is right. Joe does not yet understand which weaknesses are limiting.

"OK. So some of these are not necessarily limiting weaknesses, Joe. Some are allowable. Weaknesses are only limiting if they genuinely stop you from performing at your best. Weaknesses that do not impact your ability to do your job are allowable, so maybe you need to be a bit easier on yourself, Joe. That said, how do you think you could manage the consequences of these weaknesses?"

"Well I guess I need to work out which are allowable and look for ways to call on the strengths of those around me to compensate for those which aren't. I need to give this more thought, but *Developing Others* is probably a limiting weakness. The rest may be allowable," Joe responds in a tone that seems to lack his characteristic decisiveness.

"Good insight. How about the next area of performance risk: strengths in overdrive? Let's work through an example. In our previous session, you mentioned your *Decisiveness* strength going into overdrive. Can you think of a time where you have used your *Decisiveness* strength and it hasn't yielded the result you expected?"

"I can think of a good example," Joe responds immediately, intrigued by this concept. "In our last management meeting, we were discussing what to do about a big client that has recently restructured into multiple divisions. We currently have one account manager responsible for all sales for this client, but Mark suggested we consider alternatives, for example, having different account managers for each line of business. I was quick to pass judgement in this case, as I think Trevor, the current account manager, is doing an excellent job managing the account.

"However, now I wonder if this is the right decision, as the client has communicated that it will have different recruitment leads for each division and I'm not sure Trevor can service all these people effectively."

"So what will you do differently if a similar situation arises in future?" asks Richard.

"I will spend more time thinking about whether it is appropriate to use my *Decisiveness* strength," replies Joe, whose mind is already playing over similar scenarios in the recent past. "I'll consider whether I can dial up one of my other strengths, my *Common Sense* strength, for example, instead. I'll listen more actively to what others are saying and consider calling on one of my more people-oriented colleague's strengths. If none of this leads us to where we need to be, I'll press the *Decisiveness* button," he concludes.

"So, to summarize, you will flex your style and your strengths to get the most out of each situation, keeping you and the team on the path of possibility. You will need to practise this behaviour if you are to stay on this path though, Joe. The thing about habits is that bad ones are far easier to keep than good ones. The good news though is that new habits are easy to create, and that all you need to do to embed new habits is to intentionally practise them regularly for several months.

"Great, now let's talk about the final area of performance risk: sources of interference. It will help here if you are actually aware of what these are – internal and external – and how you can use your strengths to deal with them more effectively," Richard presses on.

Joe, trying to depersonalize the conversation, immediately starts to list the challenges the organization faces. He explains that one of his challenges is that Tiger doesn't have a clear strategy for dealing with Dragon Jobs, its biggest rival in Europe. Dragon had a much more established brand, particularly in the UK, Europe's most lucrative online jobs market. He also cites relationship problems in the team and Robert's departure to Dragon as additional problem areas he needs to tackle.

"So, to clarify...," says Richard, striding across Joe's office to a flip chart, where he lifts up a pen and gets ready to write.

"You, as the leader of this organization, are facing several challenges. These are:

1. Sales are 25% behind target.
2. Several major accounts have not renewed contracts.
3. Relationships between colleagues are poor. There's a culture of mistrust and politicking.
4. The business's top performer has left to join your main competitor.
5. The business has no clear strategy for dealing with your main competitor.
6. You currently have no clear strategy for salvaging this year's performance and your boss has asked you to come up with one.
7. You are unable to use pay or performance-related bonuses as an incentive to drive your team's performance.

"Anything else?"

Joe leans back in his chair, hands behind his head, looking thoughtfully at the list on the flip chart. Seeing his challenges there, so clearly stated, is surprisingly comforting.

"No, that about sums it up," he replies.

"OK. Have you spoken to your leadership team about these challenges?"

"Well…," Joe says slowly.

"Kind of, but maybe I haven't communicated these problems with enough urgency, or in a way that encourages the team to come back with solutions. Maybe, if we did this as a group exercise, drawing on each of our strengths, we'd find a way forward," he continues.

"Good. So we are now ready to clarify a source of internal interference that appears to be frustrating your progress," points out Richard. "In order to achieve the goals we discussed last week, you will need to stop believing you need to resolve all the challenges yourself and engage the whole team in finding solutions," continues Richard.

"We could, but is that going to help me work around the pay freeze dilemma, Richard? I'm not sure you understand how big a deal a pay freeze is in a commission-based culture. I know the goals we set last week are important. I know that textbook management says to focus on the long term. But I don't work in a textbook. I work in the real world and this short-term pay freeze thing is a real problem, Richard. I need to deal with it," asserts Joe, his *Decisiveness* strength kicking in.

"OK. Let's look at the short term first then, Joe. Remember what your short-term goal is?" Richard responds, calmly.

"Profiling the strengths of my team and setting them stretching goals," Joe remembers.

"Do you think that focusing on this, enabling your team to tap into what naturally energizes them, might help them to understand that this is a short-term pain that can be overcome by excellent teamwork?" Richard asks.

"Some of them, perhaps," replies Joe, looking out towards his team, as if trying to work out which of them, if any, would really buy into this.

"Another good insight, Joe. Different people will react to the news about the pay freeze in different ways, depending on their personality, strengths, values and how they are told about it. It's going to be important to listen to all of their views and opinions. Do you agree that understanding more about their strengths will help you to work out how to tell them, and, more importantly, will help you to bring the full power of their combined strengths to the table to find a solution to this situation?" Richard asks, slowing down his speech as he comes to the end of the sentence.

"Yes," Joe replies, almost before Richard has finished the sentence.

"So, let's ask them to complete Strengthscope360^{TM} profiles, and once we understand more about them, why don't I make the focus of the next management meeting finding a solution to these pay freeze problems?" concludes Joe.

"Great idea – but maybe you can rephrase that as a more stretching goal and think about the outcome of the meeting being the capturing of a compelling vision that aligns everybody's needs and priorities and describes what this organization will look and feel like once you've solved all these challenges. Crack this and you've cracked your 'motivating without money' dilemma," suggests Richard.

Joe looks at Richard and the vision of the broken elastic band from last week's session enters his head.

"I'll think about it," he replies.

"Great!" Richard concludes, realizing it is time to move Joe onto another subject.

"Going back to the last session, you mentioned an idea for a project with your kids. How's that going?" he asks.

"Well the idea was to combine some of my strengths to find a project that would create some happy memories for Harry and Amelia. You hit a nerve last week when you said being strong was not the same as being self-sufficient. It's a nerve my soon-to-be ex-wife has a habit of hitting too. So I've been thinking about what their strengths are, what they're good at that they enjoy doing.

"Harry is very creative. He loves making things look nice. Amelia is more interested in how things work than what they look like. This can lead to arguments. It probably hasn't helped that over the years I've tried to encourage them both to be good at everything, asking Harry to be more like Amelia and Amelia to be more like Harry. All they seem to do is bicker and compete for my attention. What they do have in common though is a deep love for nature. So we came up with the idea of working together to set up our own little ecosystem in the form of a tropical fish tank. It plays to everyone's strengths, gives them an opportunity to learn about biology, maths, geography – and to be creative. It also means they'll finally have pets – something they've both been craving for years.

"Brilliant! And Lynette, what does she think?"

"Oh, the aquarium thing was kind of her idea. I'd been going down the line of joining them to the same gym as me but we got talking and came up with this idea, which we both think is much better.

"Anyway, we agreed a budget for the aquarium and I am going to introduce the idea to the kids this weekend. It's my turn to have them.

"That's if I have the energy," adds Joe.

"There is so much going on at work that by the time it's the weekend, I'm exhausted. I consider it an achievement these days if I simply manage to keep them fed and stop them from killing each other."

"So, how can you top up your energy, Joe? How can you use the sort of accelerators we use in business to energize you in your personal life? There will be such forces in your personal life too, things, people, activities that give you energy. For me they include spending time with my family and watching sport. What might be the equivalent for you, Joe?" inquires Richard, aware that a lack of energy is a very real source of internal interference for Joe, which could become a performance risk if not dealt with intentionally.

"Well, I used to go to the gym regularly. And years ago, before we had children, I ran a marathon. That was amazing. Even though I spent four hours every day training, I still had enough time and energy to do everything else. And the kids, spending time with them feels good – or it used to, before this ridiculous attention-seeking behaviour started," admits Joe.

"So, how much time have you spent at the gym recently?" probes Richard.

"Almost none. I haven't been to the gym since Lynette and I separated," Joe replies, looking down at his feet. Bringing his gaze up, he leans back in his chair, staring thoughtfully across to the park where a group of children are playing.

"Perhaps I need to get back into my regular workout routine," he adds tentatively.

"It's all about personal choice," Richard responds encouragingly. "It is clear to me that your energy at work is adversely impacted by a lack of exercise, but you will need to make a conscious effort to change the energy sapping routine you have established over the past year or so. You will need to be intentional. Are you ready to do this?" he pushes.

"I think so," replies Joe, wondering how on earth he is going to find the time. "I'll update you next time we meet."

"And the next time we meet, we'll review your progress against your goals and take a look at how to deepen this new habit *Sharing Vision*, moving onto the next habit – *Sparking Engagement*. Then it's decision time. Will you be seeing more of me, or will it be our final session?" concludes Richard.

"I think you know the answer to that, Richard. You can't leave me high and dry on having shared a vision, with no knowledge of how to engage people in delivering it. I need to see this through now," Joe responds looking directly at Richard.

"Good. I'm pleased. Oh, and don't forget to fill in your Learning Journal!" Richard concludes, smiling as he shakes Joe's hand.

 Joe's Learning Journal entry

1. I can overcome limiting weaknesses by dialing up my own strengths. I need to dial up my *Strategic Mindedness* strength far more over the coming weeks; this organization needs a clear direction. I also need to dial up my *Leading* strength to build a more cohesive team.

2. I've been focusing too much on tasks and results recently, at the expense of people and relationships. Some of my strengths are clearly in overdrive and putting this organization's performance at risk! I need to call on some of my team's strengths to help here and profiling the team will help me to understand who can help where. At the same time, I need to intentionally build into my daily routine the habit of *Developing Others*.

3. There are so many things putting my, and my team's, performance at risk – "sources of interference", as Richard puts it. Creating and sharing a vision will help address some of the external sources of interference. My main internal source of interference is lack of personal energy. I am going to do something about this. I am committing to going back to the gym three times a week.

4. Breaking the news about the pay freeze is going to be tough. If I crack this *Sharing Vision* habit though, and involve the team in finding solutions and creating a longer-term vision they can truly believe in, it may lessen the negative impact on morale and performance.

Chapter 4

Habit 2: *Sparking Engagement (optimizing others' strengths)*

In which Joe practises optimizing the strengths of others and takes action to reduce performance risk...

"So, guys, there it is. My strengths, weaker areas and strengths in overdrive revealed; the issues this organization is facing clarified and an invitation for you all to identify your strengths and performance risks, using the Strengthscope360™ profiler.

"The goal of the next management meeting is to draw on our collective strengths to really nail a compelling vision that aligns all our strengths and describes what this place is going to look like and what we want to achieve as a business. So a description of what success looks like," concludes Joe, pointing to the whiteboard on which he has just shared the challenges identified with Richard at his last session.

"Any questions?" he adds, wondering who is going to be the first person to point out the risks of ignoring weaknesses.

"Yes," pipes up Sally.

"Why wait until the next management meeting to agree on this picture of success? Why don't we all go complete this assessment now, have the meetings over the next three days and end the week with another meeting to keep momentum going?"

"Because we've got jobs to do," interrupts Phil. "How is doing all this stuff going to help us close the gap we have between where we are now and where the business plan says we should be? It's nearly the end of the quarter. We need to make our numbers. If we have to do this development stuff, can't it wait until next quarter?"

Joe is shocked to hear the two voices he had been listening to in his head over the previous few weeks take on a life of their own in the boardroom, embodied in real people – his management team. The pros and the cons of focusing on strengths; the fear of not fixing problems and weaknesses first: it was fascinating listening to it all being played out before him. Hearing who said what gave him helpful clues as to what his team was made of, where different areas of strengths lay, who would choose to go with a more positive mindset and who would struggle. All was not what it seemed, he realized.

"OK, guys, this is an interesting discussion.

"Sally, completing the assessments now *is* possible. The results will not be back before the end of the month though as we need to give colleagues the time to respond. Just as I invited you all to complete the assessment about me, you will be asked to nominate a number of colleagues to complete it about you. There's no reason why we can't end the week with a meeting about the vision though," suggests Joe.

"And Phil, understanding our individual and collective strengths is really going to help us to get our teams engaged and close the gap you're talking about. Once we know our strengths, stretching them takes very little extra time. We just start practising new behaviours every day. The type of behaviours I'm talking about include," Joe moves over to the flip chart and bullets the following:

- Finding new ways of performing current tasks that utilize our key strengths
- Getting involved in activities beyond our roles where we can make a positive difference using our strengths
- Helping and training others in our areas of strength
- Using our strengths in different situations.

"Doing these sorts of things actually creates positive energy. It doesn't drain you at all. I know. I've been practising some of these. For example, I'm trying to use my *Initiative* strength now in this meeting, a strength I usually reserve for other places. I'm finding that thinking and acting in this new way is helping me get through my 'to do' list quicker than ever before. I'm even finding time to go to the gym again," Joe explains.

"Isn't this just another way of saying 'do more with less' to an already overstretched team?" cuts in Raj.

"Well, that's one way to look at it. Some would say that 'do more with less' is the definition of innovation. I think most of our staff would like to be thought of as innovators. I guess the thing to point out is that stretching your strengths is not about working harder. It's about working smarter, and that if they're doing work focusing on what comes naturally, then they will feel more energized. I know I do."

Joe pauses. It seems as if everybody is listening. He decides to go one step further. Turning to the flip chart, he asks:

"What's the alternative?"

Drawing a line down the middle of the page, he labels one side "Limitation" and the other "Possibility".

"As I see it, there are two alternatives. We can either keep on the path of limitation, or move to the path of possibility."

Leading a brainstorming session, he completes the sheet as shown in Table 1.

Table 1

Limitation	Possibility
Negative uncooperative attitude	Positive "can do" attitude
Bad morale	Engaged staff/upbeat atmosphere
Poor customer service	Excellent customer service
Silo thinking	Collaborative thinking
Poor performance	Improved performance
Unwanted turnover	Talent retention
Lack of growth	Growth

"OK. I think I've done enough talking for one day. That's something else I want to change around here by the way. From now on, I want to contribute less to these meetings and for you all to contribute more. I can provide the 'what' but we all need to work out the 'how' together. There's one more thing I want to say though – well, ask, actually.

"I want to ask you all to go away and think about what it would feel like if you were doing the best possible work that you could, that you were fully optimizing your strengths. I want you to think about professional athletes and how they get better at what they do best. They take regular practice to push the boundaries and build their physical and psychological strengths. I am offering you all the opportunity to do that here, to identify your areas of potential excellence and test your limits. I have research you can read, if you want, that shows that this approach works in business and that it will help us to overcome these issues, and to sustain progress.

"Now, a show of hands please, who wants to keep momentum going, as Sally suggested, and have the next meeting, the goal for which is to define our vision, or picture of success, on Friday and who wants to take another week? Hands up for Friday."

There are two hands in the air, belonging to Sally and Gwen. Raj and Phil's hands are firmly under the table. Both look defiant. After a long pause Mark sighs, "Well, we cannot let it be said there is a gender divide in this leadership team. It does make sense. We do need to do something. Why wait?" raising his hand.

"Good. Raj and Phil, are you happy to give it a go, even though you're not 100% convinced? Your healthy scepticism will give us balance. Shall we go for it?" leads Joe.

Raj and Phil agree to do so.

"OK then. Please make the time to complete your Strength-scope360^{TM} assessments for tomorrow morning to get the ball rolling. I'll schedule individual meetings with you all for the end of the month with Richard, and with myself. We'll meet on Friday to nail the picture of success and look at how to get some quick wins," Joe concludes, before asking Raj and Phil to stay behind to discuss their concerns with him in more depth.

*

It is Thursday. Joe is updating Richard on the week's events.

"Well, Joe. This is good news. You've made a great start. Once you've identified the strengths of your leadership team, you'll know better how to optimize them. This is a key behaviour associated with all the Stretch Leadership™ Habits. Even better news is that you're already practising some of the behaviours associated with the *Sparking Engagement* habit," reflects Richard.

"I am?" inquires Joe.

"You are. The behaviours associated with *Sparking Engagement* are: empowering people; encouraging openness (and being open to challenge); inspiring learning; and valuing feedback.

"Let's look at the first of these: empowering people. This involves sharing information and enabling people to decide how best to meet their own performance goals. It means delegating responsibility to staff throughout the organization. Sounds like you've already set the scene for this to start happening with the leadership team?" Richard prompts.

"Yes. So next I need to encourage them to pass it down the line, I guess," Joe responds. He is feeling rather pleased with himself.

"Yes. How are you going to do this though? How can you motivate your staff to bring the power of their ideas into work?"

"I'm not sure. I suppose I need to get out of their way and just let them get on with things," ponders Joe.

"Exactly. You need to trust them and to show them that you trust them. This is the foundation of effective empowerment. You need to establish clear expectations and boundaries, then allow people to find their own path to their outcomes. This will enable them to take ownership of problems, solutions and results.

"If someone is new or inexperienced, you might need to give them more direction or guidance, but once they've gained experience, it's important to trust them and delegate responsibility, as well as more important tasks, to them. Without this level of trust and delegation, it will be tough to build a positive, innovative culture and you and the other members of the team won't be able to get on with the really important role of effectively leading Tiger towards its goals," advises Richard.

"So, trust then?" summarizes Joe, keen to move the session on.

"That's right. Onto the next behaviour then: encouraging openness. You told me that you were open to the challenges raised by team members at the last management meeting. To truly engage the leadership team, and the wider team, Joe, you need to be totally consistent. You need to create an open and respectful working environment where people feel like they can share their ideas and their views without criticism or judgement." Richard senses Joe's need for speed learning this session.

"OK. Surely a change of culture like that will take forever though, Richard? I don't know whether you've noticed, but I don't have a lot of time to play with here," Joe interjects.

"Well, you do have a wider team remember?" Richard responds.

"Soooo…" Joe drags the word out to give himself thinking time.

"Ah, I get it, I can give one of them a goal to make this happen, maybe they can put in place practices and mechanisms to change the way we do things," he concludes.

"Good plan. How will you ensure that learning is always practised and becomes 'the way you do things around here' then? How will you ensure that all staff have challenging opportunities that will help them grow?"

"Well, I guess I need a starting point. I need to understand all of their strengths, skills, aspirations and values in order to help them find challenging opportunities," Joe reflects.

"Go on," encourages Richard.

"And then I need to empower one of the leadership team to make this culture change happen. It's another stretch project isn't it?" smiles Joe.

"See, you're already getting the hang of the first behaviour; you've just empowered two members of your team!" laughs Richard as he thinks, not for the first time that day, how much he loves his job.

"What are you going to do about the final behaviour, valuing feedback?" he probes.

"Well, it immediately springs to mind that we already practise this behaviour in various ways. Getting the leadership team to undertake the Strengthscope360™ exercise demonstrates we value feedback. Maybe we should extend it across the whole organization.

"We also have a staff engagement survey and a customer feedback survey," Joe advises.

"Can you think of any other ways you can canvass opinions or feedback?" Richard pushes.

"Well, I guess we could survey colleagues in our other offices around the world about their perception of our performance and culture in the UK office," Joe replies beginning to look distracted.

"Good. One other idea I've seen work is carrying out 'stay' interviews as well as the more traditional style 'exit' interviews. Finding out why key talent stays here and clarifying any of their concerns," Richard adds.

"I'll remember to try that, if any of our talent stays," Joe jokes, dryly.

Richard, recognizing the giveaway sign of Joe's defensive use of humour, realizes that Joe is in danger of getting too far beyond his comfort zone too quickly. He decides to round up the session.

"I look forward to hearing how the meeting goes tomorrow. Enjoy the rest of today because from tomorrow you're going to have to start turning the heat up. Once you've got these guys engaged, you need to start practising the third Stretch Leadership™ Habit – *Skilfully Executing*. Remember, a habit is not a habit until it becomes second nature. To begin with, you have to purposefully implement a behaviour. It is only conscious and persistent repetition that turns a behaviour into a habit. This involves the behaviour of stretching people to their limits – but no further – and ensuring results get delivered. Something we'll discuss at our next session," Richard says firmly as he moves towards the door.

Joe returns to his desk and smiles as he sees an elastic band discarded on his desk. His smile fades as he realizes that he has not spoken with Richard about breaking the news of the pay freeze. Remembering Richard's advice from the previous session, he relaxes a bit, deciding to fill in his Learning Journal whilst things are still fresh in his mind.

 Joe's Learning Journal entry

1. Four key behaviours are associated with the *Sparking Engagement* habit: empowering people; encouraging openness; inspiring learning; and valuing feedback. To make these real, it is important that I optimize my own strengths and those of my colleagues too.
2. To embed all these behaviours, we need to create a culture where people feel valued, involved and trusted. I think Gwen will be brilliant at helping us to achieve this and I'm going to ask her if she'd like it as a stretch project. If she does, I'm going to offer to support her in creating and implementing a plan based on encouraging a highly motivating environment that ensures we are the sector's employer of choice, regardless of the pay freeze.
3. I'm confident that we're already doing a lot of this. We're just not letting people know we value it. I'm going to make a conscious effort to notice where and when we are doing this every day and to encourage and celebrate it. That will help to keep us on the path of possibility.

Chapter 5

Habit 3: *Skilfully Executing (strengths-based culture)*

In which Joe practises stretching the limits and reinforces a strengths-based culture...

I t is Friday morning and Joe is intent on practising the new behaviours he has learned to help spark engagement. He thanks everybody for completing their Strengthscope360^{TM} assessment and asks each for feedback about how they felt after completing the assessment. Most agree that it felt energizing. Some admit that they are a little anxious about the feedback they'll be getting from the colleagues they'd invited to contribute.

"Tell me about it!" he laughs. "I'm still recovering from what you all said about me. In fact, let's not talk about it. Let's get cracking with crystallizing our picture of success – what this organization will look and feel like in let's say one year's time, and what we will have achieved," he continues.

Working through an exercise Richard had shown him, Joe facilitates a discussion, with the help of Post-it notes, culminating in the following succinct statement:

"Tiger created the future of recruitment."

Working with the team to visualize and list what people would be saying about them when they had achieved this, what they would be doing, what other signs of success there would be to signify that they had achieved their goal, was like lighting a firework. Well, for most of the team.

"That was a brilliant session, everybody, thanks for contributing so openly. Oh, and by the way, I was joking about your feedback being hard to swallow. I found it very enlightening and believe it's helping me to get my act together and become a better leader. I think you'll be surprised about how helpful the insights you give each other are too," Joe concludes.

"Joe. I need a word," Phil states flatly as the others head to the door.

Phil was the only member of the team who had not completed the Strengthscope360™ assessment. Observing Phil's contribution – or lack thereof – during this session, Joe knows what he has to do.

"Sure, Phil, come this way," he responds calmly, leading Phil to his office.

An animated and open discussion about Phil's comfort zone begins. Phil lists too many reasons why he cannot move beyond his comfort zone. He questions the reality of a stretch zone where people do their best work, or the need for one. He claims Joe's actions will push the entire team over the edge and into burnout territory. He also emphasizes the need for the team to get on with the "day job", rather than being distracted by "all this culture change and development nonsense".

Thirty minutes later, Phil emerges from Joe's office. The two have come to an agreement. While they concur that Phil has the right skills for the position, which is why he was recruited, his strengths and mindset do not lend themselves to easily adapting and thriving in the type of culture Tiger is encouraging. Phil enjoys the comfort zone and is simply not willing to do what is necessary to go beyond it. He has always dreamed of setting up his own business, one that fitted in around his family and lifestyle. Joe hands him a lifeline – a day a week as financial advisor to Tiger Recruitment for a period of three months, with an opportunity to be introduced to other organizations in the Tiger network. Phil is, in his own quiet way, very pleased with the agreement he has struck with Joe. Joe is frankly relieved, especially as he is confident that he can draw on the strengths of other members of the Finance team to cover for Phil's departure.

*

"You have the makings of a very powerful team here, Joe," reassures Richard as he concludes his summary of the management team's Strengthscope360^{TM} profiles.

"Between you, your team covers almost every area of that strengths wheel we talked about and, you have the right mix of strengths to improve the performance of this business. The not so good news is that you lack a team member with *Developing Others* as a core strength. This may become a limiting weakness if you do not address it intentionally.

"The next step is to look at these people to see where they fall in the passion–performance grid," advises Richard as he brings a graphic up on his screen.[1]

---

[1] See Appendix, The Stretch Toolbox, 1.6. Passion–Performance Grid.

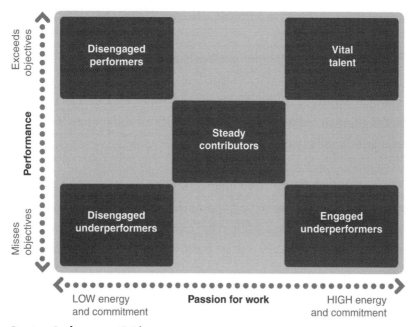

Passion–Performance Grid

The clues given at the meeting earlier in the week, and the knowledge provided by the Strengthscope360™ profiles, make placing the management team members on this grid an easy task for Joe. The outcome though is a little worrying. With Phil (who Joe had once thought of as his heir apparent) gone, Mark falling into the disengaged under-performer area and Raj an engaged underperformer, Joe for the first time that week feels under pressure. Reminding himself of the need to choose a more positive mindset by asking himself what is good about his team currently, he notes that at least Gwen is a steady contributor and Sally is vital talent.

"How would it feel to have all members of your team sitting up there with Sally – a team of vital talent?" asks Richard.

"I have no idea, but if they were, I sure as hell wouldn't be sitting here having this conversation with you, Richard!" jokes Joe.

"Do you think it is possible?" pushes Richard.

"I think it's unlikely, given recent performances, but I'm guessing you're going to tell me that it is and that it's all about stretching their strengths," replies Joe.

"Correct. By positively stretching each team member, aligning their strengths to their roles, setting appropriate goals and projects, there is no reason why your leadership team cannot all be contributing at the level that Sally is. The key is to set positive – not negative – challenges, Joe.

"What do you think the difference is between positive stretch and negative stretch, Joe? How will you know if you're on the right track?" asks Richard.

"I guess negative stretch is asking them to change too quickly. There'll be signs that they are hurting," Joe responds, rubbing the back of his neck as he leans back in his chair.

"Kind of, but not quite. Whenever we try something new, it hurts a bit to start off with. If it doesn't, we're not really stretching outside the comfort zone. It's more about whether you're asking them to stretch in areas of strength or not, and whether they're feeling adequately supported.

"Positive stretch is usually in line with the person's strengths and needs the right level of support. Support should be provided from you, their manager, but can also come from co-workers, coaches, mentors and others. It also means intentionally building a positive, open work environment which encourages risk-taking, agility, teamwork, and shared learning. Negative stretch is unsupported challenge in an area of weakness. Like expecting a fish to swim out of water," concludes Richard.

"OK. So what do I need to do next then, Richard?" asks Joe, picking up the pace.

"Well, you need to have some firm but supportive conversations with those guys and encourage them to set their own goals, while you focus on staying on course with yours. One thing that will help you stay in positive stretch is to take a good look around at who you have to help you. The best leaders I've ever worked with have not just sought support from coaches. They've also informally appointed support from their personal and professional networks," replies Richard.

"What sort of support?" asks an intrigued Joe.

"Well, different types from different people. Typically they've turned to someone in a similar situation to themselves, with similar interests and career aspirations to support them as a collaborator; to someone with strong interpersonal skills and networks as a connector; to someone strong on empathy and encouragement to provide emotional support, kind of like a counsellor; to someone strong on optimism for encouragement; and to someone within the industry, steeped in experience, for long-term support, guidance and wisdom, kind of like a mentor. It's like selecting your own personal development board really[2]," Richard explains.

---

[2] Based on "Personal Board of Directors" concept introduced by Clifton, D.O. and Nelson, P. (1992). *Soar with Your Strengths*, New York: Dell Publishing.

"Shall we look at who might be on your board?"

Twenty minutes later, reviewing the strengths of those around him with Richard's help, Joe has written the following in his notebook:

Name	Role on Development Board
Ahmed (colleague from a previous role)	Collaborator
Mark	Connector
Gwen	Counsellor
Lynette	Encourager
Kelly	Mentor

Joe is reeling with shock from the realization that his estranged wife's strengths make her the perfect encourager and that Kelly's strengths and experience make her the perfect mentor. Strangely, he is more at ease with addressing the unfinished business relating to the management team's absence of vital talent, not to mention the *Developing Others* strength, than he is to asking these two for support. "How are you feeling, Joe?" asks Richard.

"Positively stretched, Richard! I'm very curious to find out what people's reactions are going to be to their profiles, and to what their suggestions are going to be around aligning their strengths to roles. Kind of like Sally yesterday, I'm just keen to keep up the momentum, to move from action to agility," Joe responds, remembering the expedition analogy Richard had shared with him in their first session.

"I'm also thinking that I should ask the rest of the team to form their own personal development boards too. I think it's a powerful way to help keep yourself on track, or can be if you have the right support around you," he adds.

"Good idea. Let's add that to the Strengthscope360™ review sessions we have with each of them then," suggests Richard, as he prepares for the first such meeting with Mark. "We could simultaneously introduce them to the first behaviour linked to the third habit of *Skilfully Executing*".

"Which is?" enquires Joe.

"Setting clear, stretching and achievable performance expectations and ensuring people are held accountable to these," advises Richard.

"Well, I'm ahead of the curve here. I've already got that covered. What do I need to do next to be able to execute things skilfully?" asks a smiling Joe.

"Encourage the rest of your leadership team to adopt this behaviour and continue to take decisive action to deal with performance shortfalls and unproductive behaviour, just like you did with Phil. Encouraging the rest of the leadership team to do likewise too, of course," Richard responds quickly, recognizing Joe's eagerness to learn as much as possible this session.

"OK," acknowledges Joe.

"Regularly reviewing progress to stay on track and maintain momentum is the third behaviour linked to *Skilfully Executing*. Inviting regular input from employees and other stakeholders and building this into decisions and plans is the final behaviour. Shall we get to it?" asks Richard, as he and Joe prepare to enter their first one-to-one Strengthscope 360™ feedback session with Mark.

*

It is the next management meeting. Each member of the team has met with Richard and with Joe to look in detail at how to optimize their strengths and reduce their performance risks. At these sessions, Joe had been sure to encourage the new behaviours he was himself still learning, setting each of them specific goals. He had also taken some pretty decisive actions to deal with performance shortfalls within the team.

The team is about to find out…

"So, the good news is that we have a good spread of strengths and skills to help us get back on track. Perhaps you'd each like to share with us your feedback and plans?"

One by one, each member of the team shares their key strengths, observations about performance risks and plans about their goals and projects. Things are going really well. Raj is to head a stretch project around networks. Gwen is to lead one looking into culture and talent. Having identified that a key member of her team, the HR manager Jane, has *Developing Others* as a strength, she is to share a lot of this work.

There comes a surprise though when it's Mark's turn.

"So, do you want to tell them or shall I?" asks Mark, looking at Sally.

"Go for it. I'll join in where I need to," Sally replies after a pregnant pause.

The tension is palpable. The team is still reeling with shock that Phil is no longer with them. They are wondering "What now?"

"So, guys. This is goodbye. It seems that I am not a natural Operations Director," he states solemnly.

Sally, following his lead, stands up too. She announces:

"And it's goodbye from me also. Seems that I am not a natural Sales and Marketing Director."

Raj and Gwen are stunned. They do not know where to look or what to say. They had been carried away by the positive wave of their own reviews and were just beginning to think that this stuff worked. They really had not expected this.

"Don't worry though. We're both sticking around, supporting each other in our existing roles, with a view to maybe swapping roles in the next quarter if that is what we think is the best thing to do for the business," explains a playful Mark.

Gwen and Raj are visibly relieved, Joe and Sally amused, as Mark goes on to explain more.

"You see, when I got my profile it all became obvious. My top three strengths are *Relationship Building, Flexibility* and *Collaboration*. I'm really people-focused. Reading that was one of those lightbulb moments; I realized how much I missed using these strengths in a sales environment. I realized that I was frustrated in an operations role, which requires different strengths," Mark shares.

"And when I got my profile, I realized that my top strengths, *Efficiency, Detail Orientation* and *Optimism*, were not being given enough space to flourish. Although I do enjoy working with people, I'm very process-driven and having sorted out all the processes in sales and marketing, I'm up for new challenges. When we had our one-to-ones with Richard and Joe, it soon became clear that there was a possible answer, a job swap. We chatted and it makes sense but we have agreed to be cautious and work more closely together over the next three months, before making any lasting changes," interjects Sally.

"And I for one am delighted to be working more closely with Sally in my natural habitat, sales and marketing. I'm in my element when networking and doing deals. Without jumping straight into strategy, I've a feeling the way to increase sales in the current environment is to drive new products through new partnership initiatives, so that's my stretch project. I know how to do this. I've done it before. I want to do it and I know that Sally's extraordinary ability to plan and execute projects, improve quality and remain positive and upbeat will serve us all better if she has the time she needs to look after realigning our processes to be more streamlined and customer-driven," enthuses Mark.

"Yes!" laughs Sally. My *Efficiency* and *Detail Orientation* strengths will enable me to work with you all to realign our processes so we can deliver more value to customers. My *Optimism* strength may be in what Joe calls 'overdrive' here but I'm really looking forward to this opportunity," she adds.

The team congratulates Mark and Sally, they are all upbeat and appear energized and high spirited about the exchange. Joe decides to remind them of a few basics whilst the mood is right.

"So. Looks like we have a plan coming together. I just want to remind us all, including myself, of a few housekeeping items … ground rules if you like. Just because Gwen and Jane are leading on the culture project doesn't mean we can sit back and watch. Each and every one of us around this table needs to start building *Developing Others* into our daily routine. This is especially important as none of us have this as a natural strength. We need to be really intentional about it if things are going to change around here.

"From now on, we all know what we're accountable for and we all know what each other's natural strengths are. We know we can call on the strengths of each other and those around us. The more we do this, the better we'll get at it.

"Let's remember, we will be a lot stronger if we work together to help each other overcome our weaker areas and other performance risks. We're going to need to do this to meet the challenges ahead, especially when we roll out the news about the pay freeze I shared with you each at our one-to-ones. The goal of the next management meeting is to decide how to communicate this to the rest of our teams in a way that will help them to accept it.

"Oh, and remember the personal development board idea we talked about at the one-to-ones? Please consider setting one up. I think it will really help us all," concludes Joe, who is really rather pleased with his team. He doesn't feel like he's lost a key member. He feels like he's found four.

Emboldened by his success, Joe decides to take the step of sharing with Kelly what he has been working on, and asking her to take on the role of mentor in his personal development board.

Having clearly defined what he wanted from her the night before, he prepares himself mentally before making the call. Whilst sharing the role of mentor and boss is not exactly textbook management technique, Joe reasons that he has far more to gain than to lose from such an arrangement. He makes the call…

"Right, Joe. I know I told you not to come to me with complaints about your team but I was not expecting this!

"It all sounds nice to do and I hear that it's getting some results but I'm not hearing enough yet. It sounds like this whole strengths thing is just going to eat into time, not to mention money. If I'm going to invest in this I really need you to show me how this is going to turn us around and help us make the numbers," Kelly summarizes.

"And have you even told your staff about the pay freeze yet?" she adds, clearly irritated.

"Not yet, Kelly. I've told the leadership team, but we've decided not to share the news more widely just yet. We want to give them something to believe in before we take away something they expect. Don't worry, we've got it covered. And we've ensured that this has not cost you anything to date, Kelly. We have financed it from existing budgets. All I ask is for you to take on the role of being my mentor and help me to better understand the trends and innovations in the US recruitment market, so I can bring the best of it over here.

"And I don't think it is down to just me to show you how this is going to turn us around. Come over and meet the team. Each of them has a story to share. Each of them is achieving some quick wins that will demonstrate how we're going to do more than just make our numbers, pay freeze or no pay freeze," Joe replies, realizing that he is actually enjoying this conversation.

"OK. I'll come. I'm making no promises Joe, but I will come and I will listen. And I will be happy to act as your mentor too," Kelly concludes.

Joe puts down the phone, leans back in his chair and looks out over the park. Smiling, he picks up his pen and journal and completes another entry.

 Joe's Learning Journal entry

1. Most people respond well to positive stretch although you have to help them overcome any initial fears and concerns about the changes they need to make to move outside their comfort zone. Once you help them to understand what needs to be achieved and make them aware of their strengths and how to use them productively, they can work out the "how" and will be more inspired to perform the job to a high standard.

2. We need to harness passion to drive performance so that every member of this leadership team can become a vital talent. The way to do this is to spot people's strengths and skills and actively develop talent and future leaders. We need to call on the individuals who have the best strengths for the task in hand and support each other to reduce areas of performance risk. I will take personal responsibility to review the finance team's talent pool to find a workaround while we hire for a replacement Finance Director.

3. Even though *Developing Others* did not show up as a clear strength for Gwen, I will check in with her to see whether this is a potential strength area for her as she seems to have a fair amount of energy for helping others learn and grow.

The fact that she spotted a strength in Jane and seems keen to help the team develop supports this insight. We shall see...

4. I need to ensure I stay, and keep the team, in positive stretch. The way to do this is to align goals to strengths and to continue to provide support.

5. Even though I've just lost the person who, just two weeks ago, I considered to be *the* key member of the team, I feel like I've re-discovered the strengths of my other team members which I saw when I first hired them. Dealing swiftly with people whose values and mindset don't match those of the organization is really important.

6. Even though Kelly has not agreed to anything yet, other than to be my mentor, I feel really hopeful that, through strong teamwork and putting our collective strengths to work, wisely, we can turn this business around and gain her support for our new vision, culture and goals.

Chapter 6

Habit 3: *Skilfully Executing (reinforcing a strengths-based culture)*

In which Joe continues to stretch the limits…

Yaaaay! Dad, it's beautiful. When can we get the fish? Can we go get them now?" gushes Harry, stepping back to look at the tropical tank he has just set up with Amelia and his dad.

"What do you think, Amelia?" prompts Joe who, for once, has noticed that his usually talkative daughter has actually gone quiet.

"I really enjoyed setting that up but I'm a little worried that we've got it wrong and if we introduce fish, they'll just die – or eat each other," she explains.

"Well, what did the book say about when to introduce fish?" Joe asks.

"To leave it three to five days for the water to settle and the plants to do their stuff oxygenating the water, or something; then to test the water for levels of pH, chlorine and other chemicals. We can take a sample to the pet shop and they will run the tests. Then, if the temperature is stable too (Dad, you're going to have to keep checking the thermometer and make sure it stays within this green safety zone), we can add our first couple of fish," Amelia explains.

"And don't forget about the lights, Dad. You need to switch the day-time light off and the night-time light on every evening, and the night-time light off and day-time light on every morning to help establish the cycle," adds Harry.

"Dad, can we come after school on Wednesday and go back to the pet shop with the water samples? PLEASE?" he urges.

"Yeah, can we?" pipes in Amelia.

"Well, if your Mum says so, I don't see why not. Don't be too disappointed if the water isn't ready though. It may take more time, but we may as well go for it," Joe answers, delighted that his kids, for the first time in a while, are actually keen to see more of him.

"Come on, let's get you home, then we can ask. I need to talk to your mum about something else anyway," Joe adds, ushering them out of the apartment and into the car.

It is the next morning. Lynette accepted Joe's offer of the role as his encourager to assist with his development, having at first joked that she wanted to take legal advice. At least, he *thought* she was joking. Now he is sitting with his coach, Richard, and is suddenly very conscious of how much he has changed in such a short period of time.

"Good. Now, let's look in more detail at how to practise the stretch habit of *Skilfully Executing*," Richard states, having reviewed developments against the targets from the previous session.

"You've already been exerting positive stretch, I can see that. It's a shame Phil was unwilling to move out of his comfort zone. I think the solution you arrived at though is good. It's also good that you agreed on the short-, medium- and long-term goals and that each leader is doing the same with their team. You're doing really well, Joe. Let's try to capture where we are now for you, the leadership team and the wider organization," Richard adds as they begin to map out goals and success measures, identifying which strengths will enable each goal.

"This is all very well, Richard," sighs Joe, looking at the road map he and Richard have been creating half an hour later. "But how am I going to get some of those guys to keep up with me? Some of them are just not as driven as I need them to be. Several also avoid making tough decisions at all costs. Plus, Gwen tells me there is a perception that Phil got fired for challenging my authority, which is just not true. But if that is what people believe, they're hardly going to start making decisions for themselves are they?"

"Brilliant!" Richard responds, leaning forward and smiling.

"Pardon?" Joe asks, after a short pause, leaning back, frowning.

"This is brilliant. You have recognized that you are dealing with a situation where you don't have all the answers and need support from others to avoid panic and burnout. This is an important skill for leaders. Well done!" Richard congratulates Joe.

Joe remains silent, looking at Richard for clues.

"What's the best thing you can do now?" prompts Richard.

"Not panic?" suggests Joe, picking up on Richard's mention of the panic and burnout zone.

"What else?"

"I don't get it," states a frustrated, tired and distracted Joe.

"Let's go back a bit to explore this idea in more detail," Richard pulls up a slide depicting the stretch zone[1], which suddenly reminds Joe of a darts board, a game he has never had much patience for.

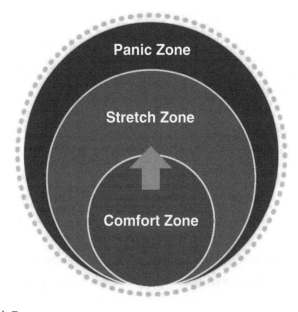

The Stretch Zone

"When you are here," Richard points to the centre labelled 'Comfort Zone', "what are you doing, exactly, and what does it feel like?"

"Well, I'm focusing on tasks, in control, doing things, achieving goals, with others following me. It feels easy – or at least it did when this approach was actually achieving goals."

[1] See Appendix, The Stretch Toolbox, 1.5. The Stretch Zone.

"And, when you are here?" Richard points to the 'Stretch Zone'.

"Well, I guess that's where I've been the last few weeks. Building strong teams, motivating people, delegating tasks and responsibilities. It's been working. We're already getting results and it feels…challenging, but more energizing. It's created a lot more choices for us, when we were feeling trapped. It's made me, and this organization as a whole, I think, feel more…effective, I guess."

"So bring me back to that discussion you had with Phil in this room, when he questioned this approach and your authority. Where in this model were you then?" pushes Richard.

"Here," Joe points to the panic zone. He is beginning to question his decision about Phil, who, since the new arrangement, has actually been far more proactive and positive. He is wondering whether he made an overly rash decision and could have avoided taking such drastic action by looking for other ways to align Phil's strengths with his role.

"Were you here? Or were you here?" Richard asks, pointing to the arrow on his screen, which he refers to as the point of stretch'.

"Ah. I get it! You're right. I created a choice, out of nowhere, when we were both feeling trapped, and it's working, even though people don't yet know it's working. Changing Phil's role from internal leader to external advisor motivated him. If things had stayed the same, he'd have become increasingly frustrated and disengaged. He may have the right strengths for the role, but his values are not aligned with the new culture here. I've found a strong replacement for him within the finance team too. So, we have everything we need to move forward."

"Good. So, where are you now?"

"I'm here," Joe points to the edge between the stretch zone and panic zone.

"And where do you want to be?"

"Back here," Joe points to the arrow that Richard has described as the 'point of stretch' again.

"And how are you going to get there?" prompts Richard.

Joe stares blankly.

Richard swipes his path of possibility slide onto the screen[2], as if to nudge Joe.

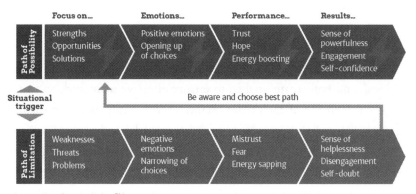

The Path of Possibility™

"Ah. I need to take the top path. I need to focus more on strengths, successes, opportunities, solutions, bringing in support and not so much

[2] See Appendix, The Stretch Toolbox, 1.2. The Path of Possibility™ Model.

on weaknesses, failures, threats and all that stuff," Joe says more confidently.

"And, if you continue to navigate along that path, what will happen to the atmosphere here, the culture of this place?" Richard pushes.

"Well, I'll be more predictable and people will begin to trust me. We'll all be more optimistic. We'll share a sense of purpose."

"Good. Back to your road map then. You state your personal goals as: strengthening your leadership, particularly your ability to engage and motivate team members; and improving your work–life balance. Your personal success measures (how you will know when you achieve your goals) are: you'll be getting positive feedback from Kelly and the leadership team; and you'll be leaving work on time at least once a week. Which of your Significant 7 strengths will enable you to achieve these goals?"

"*Leading, Strategic Mindedness* and *Initiative?*" suggests Joe.

"Good, and your team goal is: to ensure effective teamwork and positive engagement of each team member. Your team success measures are: you'll be retaining key team members and delivering the vision and strategic plan. And the staff morale will have increased (you'll know this as it will be reflected in the staff survey as well as their general behaviour, attitude and mood). Which strengths are going to help you here?"

"*Leading, Results Focus* and *Common Sense,*" Joe states this time, rather than suggests.

"OK. Now you've got the hang of it, why don't you look at organizational goals with the team? Get them to develop road maps for their teams too. If this team is to commit to your road map they need to feel like it's theirs, like they were involved in creating it. Also, take time to look at this road map again when I'm gone and think about which members of your personal development board, or your leadership team, can help you and where. Think about the strengths they have and where you can use them most effectively. Any questions?" asks Richard.

"Yes, actually," Joe responds slowly, formulating the question in his mind as he is speaking.

"You managed to bring me back from the panic zone pretty quickly there. You made it look easy. I'm not yet good enough at spotting how I can do this. Can you help me recognize when I'm tipping over (or members of my team are) and how I can feel in control again?"

"Sure. It's all about something psychologists and elite athletes call 'flow', Joe. In order to achieve flow, people need to have clear goals to provide focus. They also need the skills and strengths to do the job. They need to feel energized by it and also confident they can do the task. Very importantly, there has to be a good match between their skills and energy and the level of challenge the task provides. If there is no challenge, they are likely to quickly lose interest, become disengaged, and their performance and effort will weaken.

"Too much challenge and the reverse is true. They feel incompetent, frustrated, and out of their depth. Their performance is adversely impacted too.

"The trick is to find the degree of challenge people are currently feeling, then to create new challenges or goals that make them feel challenged and engaged, but not overwhelmed. This is exactly what you did with Phil, Mark and Sally."

"Calibrating personal, team and organizational strengths in this way keeps confidence, commitment and contribution high and we've just gone through the blueprint – this road map – to execute this.

"The main thing to remember in all of this, Joe, is not to criticize yourself or feel too anxious when you do start to feel the stretch. Feeling it means it's working, Joe. Don't forget, you're trying to break habits and behaviours you've been living for years as well as learning new ones." Richard swipes onto the screen the Stretch Leadership^{TM} Model[3] he had introduced Joe to in their first session.

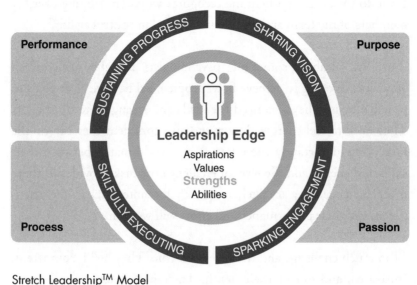

Stretch Leadership^{TM} Model

[3] See Appendix, The Stretch Toolbox, 1.1. Stretch Leadership^{TM} Model.

"Just because you now have this awareness and knowledge, doesn't mean that the new habits are going to come easily. You are still new to this way of leading, so go easy on yourself, Joe," Richard continues.

"The key is to recognize when you are edging towards the panic and burnout zone. Observe yourself for about a week and make a note of how it feels when you become agitated or overwhelmed. What are some of the things you feel? What do you see yourself doing? What do you hear yourself saying? What do people on your Personal Development Board see you doing and saying?

"For example, I know when I am in the panic zone because I feel a determination to make sure everyone knows I feel fine. So if someone asks how I am I say 'Fine. I'm fine. I'm fine'. I tend to repeat the word and want to move on and not talk about my feelings. Then on reflection I think back and realize I wasn't 'fine'. I just didn't know how to say what I was feeling or didn't feel able to say it to that person.

"A former colleague pointed out to me that this was a warning sign. You'll have similar warning signs people can make you aware of. Like rolling up your sleeves, for example," Richard smiles, watching Joe roll up his sleeves.

"Great leaders have enough humility to open themselves up and allow others in. Many actually share their triggers with those close to them and ask them to point out to them if they spot any warning signs," he concludes.

Joe is not sure what to say. He had never realized he wore his anxiety, literally, on his shirt sleeves and his former self is not at all comfortable with the idea of sharing with people that he is not actually always in control.

He thanks Richard, choosing to mull over his advice. He has other things to deal with first, like catching up on progress with the various stretch projects and working out how to communicate the pay freeze with the wider team. Kelly is coming across for the next management meeting, so he really wants to make sure the new way of working is working.

*

It is the next management meeting. Everybody has presented their team's progress against goals, apart from Gwen. It is her turn. She is aware how directly her team's work will feed into the next item on the agenda, sharing the news about the pay freeze. She seems quite calm.

"So we've accelerated the Strengthscope360^{TM} profiling and each of us will have one-to-one meetings with our staff, agreeing personal development and other goals. We've set up regular staff briefings and we've all started to make ourselves more visible within our teams – I think textbooks call it 'management by walking about'. We're all going to take our key team members to lunch once a month and we've put a call out for the wider team to suggest other ways to encourage us to all interact with each other outside of meetings," Gwen advises.

"I'm also recommending we put ourselves and all our managers on the strengths coaching programme Richard told us about in our one-to-ones, and look for more ways to coach and support each other (once we've identified our vital talent that is). Sally and Mark's peer coaching is working a treat," she continues.

"The cross-department 'lunch and learn' sessions you introduced are going really well, Gwen," Mark pitches in. "One result of the last one was that we identified and invited some of our key customers to participate in designing and piloting some of our new online offerings," he concludes.

During all this, Sally has been looking uncomfortable. She decides it's time to pitch in with what has been occupying her thoughts.

"So, if we're about to have one-to-one performance reviews in this new format, hadn't we best come up with a strategy for telling them about the pay freeze?" she asks. "I mean, how do you think they're going to take the news?" she adds.

"Well, they will all react differently. I think we can lessen the negative impact and get them to accept it if we work on this together, agree how to communicate it in a way that helps them understand that this is a temporary situation. We need to help them believe that they can shape their own future to ensure that this doesn't need to last longer than this quarter," Gwen advises.

"I agree. And I've been looking into it and it seems that we're not the only ones in this boat. Many of our competitors are laying people off as well as putting a freeze on bonuses and commissions, so if they're not happy and decide to go elsewhere, they'll soon realize they've got the best deal here, thanks to all these other initiatives we're working on," Raj interjects.

"Let's brainstorm some low cost ways to motivate people," Sally says, walking over to the flip chart.

Twenty minutes later they have a set of actions that she takes away to build into a revised reward and recognition programme, something they can all refer to during their team meetings and one-to-ones with staff.

Ways to motivate without money
1. Private notes of congratulations
2. Public recognition at all staff meetings
3. Time off for personal development or charity work
4. Free/subsidized lunches
5. Games room
6. Team rewards/activity days
7. Short breaks for top performers

Joe leaves the meeting relaxed. He decides to take ten minutes to crystallize his learning and the team's progress before leaving on time to make it to the gym prior to picking up the kids.

 Joe's Learning Journal entry

What a week! Thought I'd summarize progress as well as learning today.

1. The behaviours relating to the *Skilfully Executing* habit are crucial to move from planned goals to results. We're setting clear, challenging and achievable performance expectations and ensuring people are held accountable to these. We're anticipating and taking decisive action to deal with performance shortfalls and unproductive behaviour. We're regularly reviewing progress to stay on track and maintain

momentum. And we're inviting regular input from employees/stakeholders and building it into our decisions and plans. We're doing all of this collaboratively and although we need to be very conscious about how we do it initially, it will quickly become habit if we work closely together as a team and stick to plan.

2. Gwen's well ahead on her stretch project, creating an environment that encourages high morale, challenge and innovation. Seems that developing others was an under-developed strength for her. Working alongside Jane is really helping too. They're becoming quite a double act.

3. Sally is simplifying and streamlining our reward and recognition process to ensure everyone is provided with positive recognition and feedback and to help us break the news about the pay freeze.

4. We've created an environment of positive stretch. People are moving beyond their comfort zone. Cross-discipline teams are working on new product ideas. Some of our staff are working on projects with our key clients, helping them to formulate their recruitment strategies whilst finding out what they actually need in this challenging economic environment. Several of us in the leadership team are thinking about how we can use our strengths in stretch projects outside of work too.

5. Mark's been leading a team on a stretch project that has identified a great new product opportunity. We've handed over the findings to Sally, who is leading a team looking into how we can bring it to market before the end of the year. She is presenting the findings at the next management meeting, at which Kelly will be present. Sally and Mark are very excited about it, and their enthusiasm seems to be energizing the rest of the team. Let's hope Kelly gets it.

Chapter 7

Habit 4: *Sustaining Progress*

In which Joe recognizes achievement...

I t is the end of January. Tiger Online Recruitment is four months into its transition to a new strengths-based culture and performance management programme. The short-term goals set at the beginning of the period have largely been achieved. Processes are in place, driving the team towards achieving the company's longer-term goals. Joe is summarizing the outcome of the latest activity in the leadership team's weekly meeting, and leading an exercise to complete the organizational road map.

Kelly is present and unusually silent.

"So, we are all agreed. Our organizational goals to achieve by the end of the financial year are: strong growth in sales revenue; improvements in margins; recognition as a market leader; launching the upgraded Career Toolkit for candidates (which was identified as a way forward by Mark's team in their stretch project – well done Mark's team); and achieving outstanding client retention and engagement during the period.

"Our organizational success measures, how we know we've achieved our goals, are: we will have 100% growth in revenues with more than

15% margin; we will have won 15 new FTSE 100 clients; the Career Toolkit will be launched before the new financial year; and our client retention rates will have increased by 85% (with us having a host of positive testimonials to share off the back of our annual client survey).

"We have talked about how each of our individual strengths will enable us to achieve this, when some of us may need to dial down our strengths – such as my *Decisiveness* strength (I know you are all taking ownership for leading your areas now and I need to back off sometimes); and when we can call on other's strengths to help. For example, I can, and indeed will, call on Raj's *Efficiency* strength to ensure we are following through if I see this stuff isn't happening fast enough.

"I think this team is doing a really good job driving the UK arm of Tiger Recruitment towards making our vision a reality. It really does feel to me like we're rewriting the recruitment industry handbook, creating the future, moving beyond boundaries. Agree?" asks Joe.

There is a chorus of affirmations from around the table, with one exception, Kelly, who remains thoughtfully silent.

"So, to that temporary sacrifice we've been talking about – the pay freeze. How has the news of that gone down?" he asks nobody in particular, all the time watching Kelly closely for any clues about what she is thinking.

"Well, as we anticipated, people were not at all happy about it, but introducing ways, other than pay, to reward performance gave it as soft a landing as possible, I think," Arthur, the recently appointed acting Head of Finance, advises.

"Getting buy-in from our colleagues on our vision of 'creating the future of the recruitment industry' has helped, I think. Once they got that, and saw examples of our new reward programme in action, the grumbling quietened down a bit. They're not happy but I think we're OK for now," Mark shares.

"So long as we are true to our word and ensure this is just a temporary pay freeze," adds Sally.

Everyone around the table agrees with the exception of the still silent Kelly, silent apart from the tapping of her fingers on her tablet jotting notes, that is.

"So, now over to Sally, who is going to lead us through an exercise exploring how we can build and sustain our successes so we continue to do more with less, if you like," Joe concludes.

Sally methodically and cheerfully facilitates a discussion that reviews the skills, knowledge and learning available in-house that will enable them to launch the new Career Toolkit. Widening the discussion out, she guides the team into describing the ways in which the change in mindset, culture and, indeed behaviour have enabled them to come this far. Going further, they identify how this will enable them to expand out to the next level and deliver the first Career Toolkit in the marketplace. Mark contributes by describing the market opportunity, backing his claims up with research and statistics collected as part of the stretch project he led. He concludes by explaining how the new product will go viral if the team gets it right and draws on the power of their collective strengths and networks.

"And make no mistake, our network is already growing. We've already recruited 12 partners from the outplacement sector to help us market this. It is what everyone is crying out for. Everyone stands to win. If we can be first to market with a high quality product and our reputation for running right through it, then, well, let's just say we're going to have one monster of a kick-off party at the beginning of the next financial year!"

Joe sits back and watches his team perform. They'd only been practising this approach for six months and he'd seen individuals, and the team, shift mindset and behaviour significantly. Yet, while he had been keeping to his goal and leaving work on time at least once a week, he knew that some of the people around the table had picked up his old habit of staying late, often burning the midnight oil.

"Still, at least they're practising the new habits too," he reflects as the meeting, and the working day, draws to a close and a reflective Kelly leaves for the airport.

*

"I'm so sorry. Your water levels are not right yet. The pH, ammonia and saline levels are fine but the nitrates are high. Nitrates are toxic to fish so we need to get them down before you can introduce any," explains the sales assistant at the pet shop.

Joe sees Harry holding back tears. Before he can intervene, Amelia steps in. "How toxic? And to which fish? Surely there are some fish, somewhere in the world, that live in nitrate-rich environments?"

"I like the way you're thinking," laughs the sales assistant. "You're probably right, but even if we could select them you'd be making your job going forward very difficult. You see, successful fish-keeping is all about managing the environment. Get that right and the fish flourish. It should be called water-keeping really, not fish-keeping."

Joe smiles, as he realizes the same is true in the corporate world. Putting his hand on Harry's shoulder, he smiles at Amelia and asks: "So, what can we do to get the nitrate levels down, and how long will it take?"

"Well, a partial water change of 20%, putting the prescribed amount of this solution in, will kick start your filter into converting the nitrate back into free nitrogen gas. You can also select some aquarium plants to help with the job," the assistant advises.

"Well get to it then, Harry, go pick a plant – at least we'll be putting something alive in the tank when we get home. And Amelia, how about you take that solution and start to work out how much we need to add to a 48 litre tank? Meanwhile, I'll do what I'm best at. I'll pay."

They leave the shop subdued but hopeful. "So, kids, ready to give Mum a lesson on water-keeping?" Joe asks as they drive home, already preparing in his mind for his session with Richard the next day.

*

"So we reach the final Stretch Leadership^{TM} Habit today, Joe, Sustaining Success. Now, the way this works is that by picking up the other habits, you almost start practising this one automatically. I suggest I describe the behaviours associated with the habit and we consider whether you're already living them. Ready?" asks Richard.

"Ready," answers Joe.

"So, the first behaviour is challenging people to think and act in new and innovative ways," continues Richard.

"I think we are already well on the way to making this part of our work culture," Joe responds, smiling. "By identifying and sticking with the stretch projects and building a work culture where everyone is encouraged to use their natural strengths, we are collectively practising that behaviour. Next!"

"It sounds like a great start," smiles Richard. "The second behaviour is creating a safe environment that encourages sensible risk taking and continuous improvement," he adds.

"One of Gwen's stretch projects is tackling this. Sally and Mark's peer-to-peer coaching, leading to them swapping roles, is proof of risk taking and the way their new roles are panning out is delivering continuous improvements. We are planning to extend peer coaching to other parts of the business as a result of this success."

"Promoting a working environment that values experimentation and a commitment to learning," prompts Richard.

"Is that not the same as the last one? Experimentation? Risk taking? Are they not synonymous?"

"Not necessarily and don't forget about 'valuing a commitment to learning'. How are you demonstrating that at the moment?" clarifies Richard.

"Well, I've – sorry 'we've' – introduced pilot projects to incubate and test out new, innovative ideas, to see what we can learn from our partners. We're encouraging questions, challenge and inquiry at all our meetings. We're reviewing competitors' work and progress and trying to learn from their experiences – what's worked well and what has not. We're engaging customers in brainstorming forums and project teams to help design and/or improve products and services," lists Joe, delighted with himself as the answers stream into his consciousness.

"Gosh, quite a lot actually. I wonder what else we could be doing if we actually addressed the question directly, what was it again? Something like 'What can we do to promote a working environment that values experimentation and a commitment to learning?' Right?" he adds, his thoughts really racing now.

"Yes, exactly that," interjects an amused Richard. He's always loved the insights, energy and creative thinking generated in discussing this final habit.

"Well, I guess we could send the management team on study visits to other companies and our other offices worldwide to review practices, raise questions and gather ideas."

"We could review better practices in other sectors to see whether there are any ideas that can be incorporated, rather than reinventing the wheel," Joe is really on a roll now.

"We need to find organizations that encourage what one management book I read recently calls 'corporate entrepreneurship.' I think that could work here, as we want to encourage more employees to use their strengths to discover new ideas and turn these into innovative products and processes that help achieve our goals."

"Crikey, Richard, I could go on forever. I wonder what you've seen working though? What do you think I should be doing differently?" asks Joe.

"It sounds like you're making really good progress. Just keep doing more of the same and remind yourself to keep a positive mindset," laughs Richard.

"Oh come on, Richard, you can do better than that! Give me some ideas. What have you seen that works?" Joe is really enjoying this exchange. So is Richard.

"Well, you're already doing most of it. Managers and functional heads spending time going to team meetings of other functional areas to provide input and learn from new ideas; thorough project reviews to analyse learning, including reasons for successes and failure at various project milestones; that sort of thing.

"One thing I've seen work really well is actively encouraging employees to spend work time pondering issues and ways to solve them. Some companies, like 3M, for example, set aside specific time to enable employees to come up with and refine new ideas for product and process innovation. They also ensure their senior management team take responsibility to personally sponsor key ideas and projects to increase their likelihood of success.

"Enough?" asks Richard, amused that he and Joe seem to be swapping roles.

"Yes, for now," laughs Joe, picking up the game. "Any more behaviours I need to practise?"

"Yes. The last behaviour associated with the Sustaining Progress habit is recognizing outstanding effort and celebrating achievement (even those small wins like completing a project on time) in a fair and appropriate way.

"Talking of which, I must congratulate you on quite a spectacular fortnight since we last met. You really have made some significant changes in your leadership since the coaching began. You must recognize that?" finishes Richard, aware that time has marched on even faster than usual in his sessions with Joe.

"Want to share your learning?"

"Well, inspired by your talent for creating analogies, I think I may have come up with one of my own," Joe smiles.

"Go on…," Richard prompts, intrigued.

"Leadership is a lot like keeping fish. First of all you have to manage the environment and set everything in place to ensure the fish can each do their job properly. It's about water-keeping to start with, not fish-keeping.

"Then you have to select the right fish to live in the environment you've created. Just like you need a community of fish that work together to maintain the environment you've created – algae eaters, bottom feeders and fast fish that create water movement – so too do you need to select people with complementary strengths to maintain the corporate environment, and to keep things moving.

"And just like you can find natural solutions to put things right when they go wrong in the fish tank, so you can in the corporate world. But, just like in a fish tank, if you forget to monitor and support progress, things can start to go wrong. It's not just about setting goals at the beginning of a project. It's about proactively monitoring and reviewing them throughout.

"That is how you maintain a positive strengths-based culture that delivers success."

"Great analogy!" enthuses Richard.

"Love the bit about keeping water not fish! Think I'll be borrowing that. I read recently that the water cycle is the most important natural phenomenon on earth. It regulates our weather and the growth of food. It has no starting and no ending point but is a continuing process."

"So is your journey on the Stretch Leadership^{TM} Path. I hear you're about to complete your first circuit with an away day style kick-off party for the new financial year – further evidence that you're embedding these behaviours in your way of operating now. I know this because Kelly called me after your management meeting and asked to meet me before she flew back. We discussed taking this strengths-based approach and using it in other regions. Evidence, Joe, should you need it, that you're well on your way to meeting your goal."

"Anyway, this event is the perfect forum for you to introduce that final behaviour associated with the final Stretch Leadership^{TM} Habit of

Sustaining Progress: celebrating success," concludes Richard, with total confidence that Joe knows what to do next…

 Joe's Learning Journal entry

This stuff works. It's not a panacea though. You lose some people on the journey who wrongly assume that focusing on strengths means ignoring weaknesses. Some are put off because they think it's going to be too "happy clappy" for them too. I thought that, but actually, thanks to my team, it's all had a heavy dose of realism here.

It's hard work too – the rigid competency-based framework that we had before does not lend itself naturally to this approach, so we've had to put a lot of energy into realigning our processes. With someone less realistically optimistic than Sally leading that, the excitement could have waned, projects could have stalled and it could all go pear shaped. In fact it still could!

It does work though. And thank goodness!

Chapter 8

Postscript

In which Joe celebrates success and passes on his learning...

I t had taken Gwen and her project team some doing to pull off the biggest celebration the company had ever hosted at such short notice, but a phone call from Kelly offering some budget and her support had been the only incentive they'd needed.

The UK office had achieved 90% of its goals. Following the Stretch Leadership™ Habits, they had achieved unprecedented growth in profit and survived the pay freeze, which did indeed look like it would be short term. They had grown customer retention and engagement and had formed several valuable new strategic partnerships to help grow revenue and the customer base. They had achieved the highest levels of job satisfaction amongst the people employed in any Tiger office, anywhere in the world, in spite of the pay freeze. All this, and they had simplified and clarified their processes, ensuring they could be easily cascaded throughout the organization.

In his end-of-year address, Joe revisited the vision they had developed and shared back in the summer: *"Tiger created the future of recruitment."* He explained how the UK office had come full circle and would be continuing its journey towards building a strengths-based culture by revisiting aspirations in the new financial year. He then showed a short film Gwen and Jane had helped him to secretly produce. The film celebrated the strengths and achievements of each member of the leadership team, and the members of their teams who had proven to be vital talent.

Joe was not the only leader to spring a surprise though. Kelly made an unexpected appearance presenting the UK team with the prestigious "Tiger Team of the Year" award. She also announced that the team would be losing a leader in January. Gwen was to be seconded to the US office to lead a company-wide stretch project. Jane would be stepping up to take the position of acting director of human resources in the UK.

Joe and the rest of the team were delighted for Gwen and their US colleagues. They knew, beyond doubt, that rigid boundaries and missed targets were a thing of the past because Tiger Online Recruitment was well and truly on the path of possibility.

Or was it?...

THE END

P.S. On starting her secondment, Gwen asked Joe to provide her with his top tips for leading at full strength. His response was as follows...

 My Seven Stretch Leadership™ Lessons

1. Understand your strengths (what you're good at – or have potential to be good at – that gives you energy) and how they

can help you succeed. Align them with your values, aspirations and abilities. Gain the leadership edge.

2. Adopt the four Stretch Leadership™ Habits: *Sharing Vision, Sparking Engagement, Skilfully Executing* and *Sustaining Progress*. Positively stretch your own strengths, those of your team and those of your organization. Build skill and experience in areas of strength and challenge yourself and others to move beyond comfort zones to fully optimize strengths. Find opportunities to practice your strengths daily to ensure new, productive habits become part of your natural leadership style.

3. Create a road map detailing goals, success measures and enabling strengths. Ensure you and your team are aligned with these goals and that everybody's strengths are contributing to defined business outcomes.

4. Recruit across the full spectrum of strengths. Align people's strengths with their roles and give them a clear vision – a reason to be passionate about their work. Inspire high performance. Provide encouragement and support.

5. Choose the path of possibility. The path of limitation is unproductive and drains your emotional, mental and physical energy. The path of possibility gives a sense of positive power and enhances productive energy. It gives staff a sense of meaning and connection. It helps ensure that targets are met, again and again.

6. Focus on strengths whilst addressing performance risks caused by limiting weaknesses, strengths in overdrive and sources of interference. Moderate the volume of your own strengths and call on the strengths of others when facing these risks. Just be disciplined about the stuff that doesn't energize you but that you know needs to be done. Focus on the

benefits of doing these less savoury parts of your job to ensure risks don't derail you.

7. Building a strengths-based culture is a continuous journey. It revolves around the stages of aspiration, awareness, action, agility and achievement. Choose to take this journey. Strengths create positive energy. Strengths sustain success.

Appendix

The Stretch Toolbox

Free tools and resources to help you transform your leadership

This section, the Stretch Toolbox, contains the exercises and models referred to within the previous chapters. Please use them on your stretch leadership journey to support you in becoming a more effective leader.

Go to www.strengthscope.com/resources/leadership-tools/ to download all the tools below free of charge. Simply use the password "strengthsleader" to access all these powerful tools and to qualify for significant discounts on the Strengthscope360™ and StrengthscopeLeader™ profilers.

Downloadable leadership tools by chapter
Tools relating to Chapter 1: The Leadership Edge
- Maintaining a positive leadership mindset
- Optimizing leadership strengths, reducing risk

Tools relating to Chapters 2 and 3: Habit 1 – Sharing Vision
- Your leadership brand
- Clarifying your picture of success and priorities
- Mapping and influencing your stakeholders

Tools relating to Chapter 4: Habit 2 – Sparking Engagement
- Effective delegation

Tools relating to Chapters 5 and 6: Habit 3 – Skilfully Executing
- Managing your talent
- Finding positive stretch
- Personal development board

Tools relating to Chapter 7: Habit 4 – Sustaining Progress
- Identifying motives

Tools relating to Chapter 8 – Postscript
- Leadership success through strengths

Strengthscope360^{TM} is a multi-rater profiler in the Strengthscope® system incorporating co-worker/stakeholder feedback. This unique assessment provides brief and powerful feedback on how effectively the individual is using his/her strengths, risks to their performance and recommendations to strengthen their performance. It is used by leading organizations around the world and will improve your understanding by providing insight on:

- Feedback from co-workers and other stakeholders on how effectively you are using your strengths as well as opportunities for improvement
- Your risk areas to peak performance together with powerful ways to reduce the impact of these
- Positive ways of working that will improve your confidence, motivation and success in any situation
- How you can strengthen relationships and work more effectively with people whose strengths are different from yours.

StrengthscopeLeader^{TM} is the world's first strengths-based 360 profile designed specifically for senior managers and leaders and provides a more comprehensive multi-rater profile than our Strengthscope360™ profiler.

Unlike most other 360 profilers, StrengthscopeLeader™ doesn't just measure how effective leaders are in the behaviours they demonstrate. It also provides feedback from up to 20 raters on their unique strengths, potential performance risks and how effective they are in applying leadership habits associated with top performing leaders. Crucially, it also measures co-workers'/stakeholders' confidence in the person's ability to deliver key organizational outcomes.

1.1 STRETCH LEADERSHIP™ MODEL

How it works

The Stretch Leadership™ Model shares four essential productive habits you can purposefully embed into your behaviour to translate

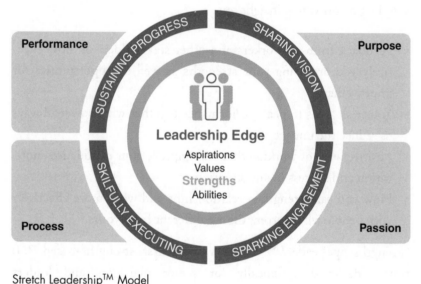

Stretch Leadership™ Model

your "leadership edge" into success. Your leadership edge is derived from the unique and powerful strengths and qualities you bring to the way you lead. Once discovered and activated, your leadership edge inspires those around you to perform at their best and achieve exceptional results.

Your leadership edge has four aspects:

1. *Aspirations* – what you aspire to achieve through your leadership and contribution; the lasting legacy you wish to leave
2. *Values* – your principles and guiding beliefs that are important to you and anchor your career and life decisions
3. *Strengths* – underlying qualities that energize us and we are great at (or have potential to become great at)
4. *Abilities* – natural or acquired talents and skills where you have an opportunity to shine.

Understanding your leadership edge is the first step in the journey to great leadership. Self-awareness must be followed by a period of stretch. The most effective leaders are masters at the art and science of stretch. They never stand still and they adopt four Stretch Leadership™ Habits – *Sharing Vision, Sparking Engagement, Skilfully Executing,* and *Sustaining Progress.* They push the boundaries of thinking and possibility, looking for new and innovative ways of doing things to achieve the organization's goals, whilst advancing their own career. In doing so, they create: a clear sense of *Purpose;* a *Passionate and engaged* workforce; clear, scalable *Processes;* and a culture of peak *Performance* and continuous improvement.

A guideline for strengthening your leadership

1. Clarify your leadership aspirations and how these relate to the organization's vision: What will it look like when you are successful? What does success mean to you? To what extent are your aspirations aligned with your personal values?

2. Discover your unique strengths using a strengths profiler like Strengthscope360™ or StrengthscopeLeader™.

3. Invite feedback from co-workers and family members who know you best on when they have seen you at your most energized and performing particularly well. This will help provide clarity on how you can bring the best of yourself to your leadership.

4. Through experience, engaging with others and education, build your skill and competence in areas of your greatest strength. Try to find leadership opportunities that match these areas.

5. Actively and consistently practise the four leadership habits by defining development goals that help you further improve those you already do well, whilst also supporting improvements in those that do not come naturally to you.

Downloadable tools available at www.strengthscope.com/ resources/leadership-tools/:

- Clarifying your picture of success and priorities
- Leadership success through strengths

1.2 THE PATH OF POSSIBILITY™ MODEL

How it works

Every day, all of us face challenges and opportunities. For leaders, choosing how to respond in any given situation provides a "moment of truth". Such "moments of truth" determine a leader's effectiveness and their impact on individuals, teams and the organization.

Most leaders, find themselves alternating between the two paths out-
lined in the following figure. Their assumptions, beliefs and interpre-
tation of a situation place them at some point on either path and
directly influence how they react to their circumstances. Other leaders have a tendency to stay more on one path than the other, based on
habitual ways of thinking.

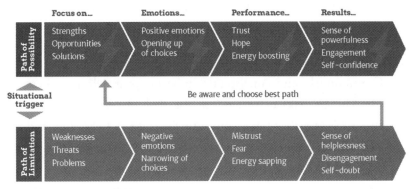

The Path of Possibility™

The lower path, the *Path of Limitation*, drives thought and actions nar-
rowed by a negative mindset that focuses on problems, issues, failures,
weaknesses and independent action. It results in fear, mistrust and
pessimism. This in turn fuels a culture of learned helplessness where
individuals and teams feel isolated and unable to progress. This self-
doubt leads to lower performance and undesirable and unintended
consequences, such as missing business targets.

The upper path, the *Path of Possibility*, is more productive. Thoughts
and actions are broadened and focused on strengths, successes,
opportunities, solutions and building collaborative partnerships.
Leadership is based on trust, hope, optimism, purpose and
energy-boosting habits. This leads to a sense of powerfulness,

positive energy, confidence and meaning at work, which fuels higher performance.

It is important to understand where you are at any point in time, and to understand the implications of your mindset on your performance and that of others who you work with. Identifying those triggers that move you to any stage of the *Path of Limitation* will enable you to recalibrate, change course and stay on the performance-enhancing *Path of Possibility*.

Guidelines to strengthen your leadership

1. Continuously and consistently draw on your self-awareness to identify the risks of staying on the *Path of Limitation*. Identify those triggers that push you onto the *Path of Limitation* and be clear on the action you will take to move back to the positive mindset of leadership.
2. Call on your strengths and those of your co-workers and stakeholders to shift gears and adopt a more positive outlook.
3. Act using the **POINT** (**P**luses, **O**pportunities, **I**ssues, **N**ew **T**hinking) method when facing tough challenges or problems. Remember the **p**luses and **o**pportunities associated with the problem, rather than becoming overwhelmed with the issues. Only then, clarify the **i**ssues and develop **n**ew **t**hinking with your co-workers to tackle these issues.
4. If your leadership style draws on the strength of critical thinking, which, when used in overdrive, can result in a pessimistic overcritical standpoint, ensure you moderate by, for example, calling on someone strong on optimism, enthusiasm or creativity.
5. Start each workday with the most energizing tasks. This will kick-start a positive mindset and increase the likelihood of moving to

and staying on the *Path of Possibility*. Delegate energy-draining tasks where possible. Where not possible, do not procrastinate. To avoid remaining on the *Path of Limitation* due to lack of energy, "start by starting".

Downloadable tool available at www.strengthscope.com/resources/ leadership-tools/:
• Maintaining a positive leadership mindset

1.3 POSITIVE BALANCE

How it works
In Asian philosophy, the concept of Yin Yang is used to describe how seemingly opposite forces are interconnected and interdependent in nature.

The central idea is that Yin Yang are not opposing forces, but complementary opposites that interact within a greater whole to give it strength and balance.

Similarly, we believe that leadership development during one's career is about balancing two opposite and interdependent dualities – optimizing strengths and reducing the effect of performance risks, including weaknesses.

Prior to the strengths-based approach to leadership development, the emphasis on employee development in most organizations was principally centred on overcoming deficits or weaknesses. A compelling body of evidence over the past two decades shows the limitations of focusing on resolving weaknesses, an approach that tends to undermine engagement, performance and confidence. Strengths practitioners recommend moving away from this deficit-oriented approach towards an approach that is focused on leaders' and employees' strengths, helping them use these to maximize performance outcomes. However, weaknesses and other performance risks should not be ignored.

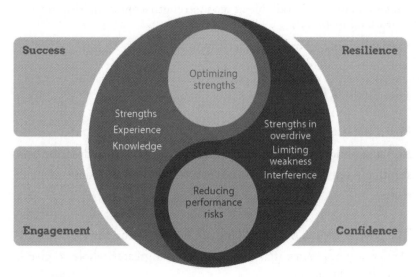

Positive Balance

Achieving success comes from ensuring a fine balance between optimizing individual and team strengths and reducing risks to performance, which we define as limiting weaknesses (as opposed to allowable weaknesses), overdone strengths (strengths that are used in the wrong way and cause unintended negative performance outcomes) and other blockers or sources of "interference", such as self-limiting assumptions and beliefs. Only by understanding and engaging with these dynamic and complementary development forces will you be able to unlock the full potential and energy of your leadership and your team.

Guidelines to strengthen your leadership

1. Adopt the 80–20 rule in your personal development: spend 80% of your development time discovering and building on your strengths with the remainder allocated to overcoming risk areas, specifically limiting weaknesses and overdone strengths.

2. Build productive habits around areas of strength, skill and experience; practise these in different situations, including unfamiliar ones, until you've mastered them.

3. Don't ignore risk areas to your performance. Uncover limiting weaknesses, overdone strengths and psychological sources of interference interfering with peak performance. Identify strategies to reduce these risks by: using strengths you do have; calling on your co-workers' strengths; and through deliberate practice to acquire new habits when these are unnatural for you.

4. Ensure your manager knows your strengths and performance risks. Invite him/her, as well as other colleagues and your wider personal network, to support you in optimizing your strengths and reducing your performance risks to accelerate your career success.

5. Apply the 70–20–10 rule when planning your development: spend roughly 70% of your time on on-the-job learning, 20% on engaging others to help you and 10% on education and formal learning. Remember that becoming a more effective leader involves continuous learning.

Downloadable tool available at www.strengthscope.com/resources/ leadership-tools/:

- Optimizing leadership strengths, reducing risks

1.4   LEADERSHIP BRAND PYRAMID

How it works

To be authentic and credible, leaders develop good self-awareness and make the most of who they are at their best. This process starts with you identifying your "leadership edge", covered in section 1.1 above. Next, transforming your leadership edge into your "leadership brand" enables you to communicate your value to others in a natural way, without it feeling forced or "salesy". Your leadership brand is what you want others to be saying about you when you're not around.

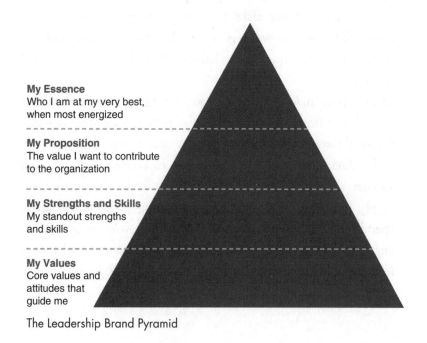

My Essence
Who I am at my very best, when most energized

My Proposition
The value I want to contribute to the organization

My Strengths and Skills
My standout strengths and skills

My Values
Core values and attitudes that guide me

The Leadership Brand Pyramid

There are four main aspects that make up your leadership brand: values, strengths, proposition and essence. Building your leadership brand and communicating it to others helps you to:

1. Differentiate yourself in highly competitive internal and external marketplaces
2. Increase your visibility in the company and make others aware of your presence
3. Ensure people have a clear sense of who you are and how to work with you
4. Become more self-confident and self-motivated as you gain further self-awareness on what you have to offer your team and the wider organization.

Strong leadership brands are not built overnight; they take a long time to evolve. They change over time too. It's worth the effort though. As with strong product brands, strong personal brands produce top results, such as improvements in demand, perceived value, reputation and results.

Guidelines to strengthen your leadership
1. When developing your brand, start with the base layer of the pyramid and identify your values – what you see as important principles in your life or standards that you follow. Build on these by next including your core strengths and skills (those things that energize you and that you are skilled at using). Think of these two levels as your "features" – important points of differentiation for you as a leader.
2. Next, develop the top two layers of the pyramid: your proposition (the value you bring to your organization); and your essence (why others would follow you or want to work with you as a leader). Focus here on summarizing and on using the language of "benefits", that is, the benefits that your leadership can bring to a project, team or organization. Remember to use language that would be natural for you to say out loud, perhaps in a job interview or when introducing yourself to a new team or boss.

3. After completing your brand, test it out on those around you who are supporting your development, such as your mentor, coach and manager, as well as trusted partners and friends outside of your work environment. Ask for feedback on what they are hearing: Is your brand clear? Does it reflect how they see you? What changes would they make to ensure your brand is more impactful and reflective of you at your very best?

4. Ensure your actions, words and leadership approach are consistent with your brand. Leaders who are consistent in their approach and who live their brands on a day-to-day basis are more trusted and respected than those who lack this consistency. Practise what you preach, be what you say you are, do what you say you will do.

5. When dealing with your manager, team and other stakeholders, find ways to communicate your brand and what you stand for, to help people know what to expect from you and what you expect from them. Invite regular feedback to check whether you are acting in line with your brand.

Downloadable tool available at www.strengthscope.com/resources/ leadership-tools/:
• Your leadership brand

1.5 THE STRETCH ZONE

How it works
The most effective leaders positively stretch themselves, their people and the organization at multiple levels. They push the boundaries of thinking and possibility, looking for innovative ways of achieving the organization's goals, whilst strengthening their own leadership and learning.

In order to stretch yourself positively, the first step is to understand the extent to which your leadership activities/tasks are currently challenging you. Your efforts can then focus on stretching in areas of strength (i.e. areas that naturally energize you and provide the greatest scope for challenge and growth), rather than areas of weakness. The aim is to move beyond your "Comfort Zone" (the zone where activities feel easy, straightforward and comfortable) and acquire new skills and experience to take your performance to the next level. The aim is to move into the "Stretch Zone" (where activities/tasks feel challenging and require you to operate at the limits of your skill, knowledge and expertise to deliver effective performance).

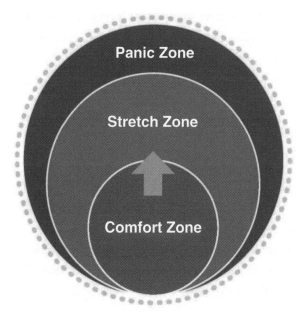

The Stretch Zone

The key to achieving positive and healthy stretch is to ensure that you do not move into the "Panic Zone". In this zone, you feel you haven't got the skills and experience to perform effectively. You feel out of your depth and negatively stressed. Like an Olympic athlete or virtuoso musician, the aim is to ensure you are continuously improving and delivering better results through growing in areas that already energize you.

Guidelines to strengthen your leadership

1. Identify areas of your leadership role where you think you are in the "Comfort Zone". Discover opportunities to stretch yourself in these areas by taking on new tasks, learning new skills or adapting your strengths and skills to lead effectively in a totally different situation.

2. Identify areas of your leadership role where you are in the "Stretch Zone". Ensure you have the relevant level of support and feedback to succeed in these areas and continue to seek feedback from others on your effectiveness.

3. Identify areas of your leadership role where you are in the "Panic Zone". Talk to your manager about these areas to get some support, delegate to others, or reallocate these tasks, at the same time developing greater skill in appropriate areas.

4. Invite your manager, mentor and others supporting your development to help you explore stretch assignments/projects within and outside your role to positively stretch your leadership strengths and take them to the next level.

5. Don't fall into the trap of spending all your time undertaking challenging, stretching tasks and activities on your own. Identify others with different strengths who can complement you and help you to deliver your leadership goals in smarter ways. Also, ensure that you spend sufficient time outside work doing relaxing and enjoyable activities and hobbies that recharge your batteries and ensure that you can sustain high levels of performance in the longer term.

Downloadable tool available at www.strengthscope.com/resources/leadership-tools/:

* Finding positive stretch

1.6 PASSION–PERFORMANCE GRID

How it works

The first step in managing the talent in your team is to choose the appropriate working style and approach that works best for each individual.

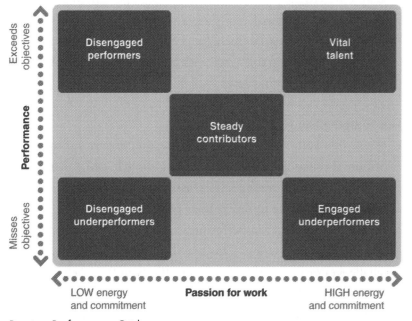

Passion–Performance Grid

To understand the best approach to take, remember that employee contribution is a function of two variables – the person's *Performance* and the *Passion* (energy and commitment) they have for their work. If we plot performance on the X axis and passion for work on the Y axis, we can identify five different talent categories:

1. Vital talent (your star performers, who will help your team to out-perform)
2. Disengaged performers (your rising stars, who, if engaged, will also help your team to outperform)
3. Steady contributors (your "hidden heroes", who, with a little encouragement, could raise their game and your team's results)
4. Engaged underperformers (the toughest to manage as they are committed to the job and company, yet their performance is below the required standard)
5. Disengaged underperformers (your most challenging team members, who need help to engage with and perform their work, or to move on to something new)

Tips to strengthen your leadership
1. Look after your vital talent by ensuring they receive strong recognition through providing challenging stretch assignments and highly visible, fast-track projects/assignments. Coach and develop these individuals to optimize their potential.
2. Work with disengaged performers to uncover the reason for the low energy and passion. This may be work-related (e.g., lack of challenge) or personal (e.g., relationship issues). Coach and support them back to high engagement.
3. Don't ignore your steady contributors. Ensure you provide them with strong recognition and challenge in areas of strength to help retain them and if they are capable and willing, coach them to move them into the vital talent category.
4. Set clear expectations for improvement to engaged underperformers. Provide coaching and skills training to build confidence and

competence. Explore alternative roles where there might be a better person–role fit.

5. Don't shy away from dealing with disengaged underperformers in a fair and firm manner. Set clear expectations for improvement and put in place short-term objectives with regular review meetings to gauge progress. Explore redeployment opportunities into a role that more closely matches their strengths and skills. Manage them out with the help of HR if there is no improvement after a reasonable period.

Downloadable tool available at www.strengthscope.com/resources/ leadership-tools/:

• Managing your talent

Glossary of Terms

Allowable weakness   Allowable weaknesses are weaker areas that don't lead to serious problems with our performance or relationships.

Emotional strengths   This group of strengths concerns how you make sense of, express and manage your emotions.

Execution strengths   This group of strengths concerns delivering results – what and how they are delivered.

"Flow"   A term used to describe peak motivational experiences and occurs when we are completely immersed or involved in an activity and are optimizing our strengths. It is also described as being in the "zone".

Interference/blockers (internal and external)   A type of performance risk that can undermine effective performance. Interference can be internal to the person (e.g. a self-limiting belief or attitude) or external (e.g. a genuine constraint in role or organization).

Limiting weakness   A type of performance that can undermine effective performance. A limiting weakness is a quality that doesn't energize us and we are not good at (and are unlikely to ever be great at).

Multi-rater   Strengthscope®'s 360 degree function – enabling up to eight raters to provide feedback on an individual's Significant 7 Strengths.

Negative stretch   Occurs where people feel overwhelmed by being stretched in the wrong way into their "panic zone" – this typically occurs where they are not supported and are being stretched in areas of weakness or non-strength.

Performance risks   There are three main types of performance risks:

- Limiting weaknesses
- Strengths in overdrive
- Sources of interference.

Positive stretch   Involves challenging people in areas of strength to enable them to learn and grow in these areas so they can achieve in the upper range of their potential, without feeling overly stressed or panicked.

Productive habit   A learned pattern of behaviour that optimizes your natural strengths, improves your effectiveness and leads to improved work outcomes.

Relational strengths   This group of strengths concerns establishing and maintaining productive relations with others.

Significant 7   The Significant 7 Strengths refer to the seven highest rated strengths within an individual's Strengthscope® profile.

Standout 3   Those strengths that an individual chooses for themselves as being most energizing to them at work based on the list of Significant 7 Strengths.

Strength   We define strengths as underlying qualities that energize us and we are great at (or have potential to become great at).

Strength in overdrive   This occurs when strengths (or a combination of strengths) are overused or used in the wrong way or at the wrong time leading to negative performance outcomes.

Strengths-focused   Strengths-focused HR and talent practices involve focusing on individuals' strengths, successes and potential to rebalance the more typical problem or deficit way of approaching talent management, including hiring, development and retention.

Strengthscope®   An online assessment system that helps energize peak performance at work. The system is the most extensive of its kind on offer today and comprises the following assessments:

- Strengthscope® Standard
- Strengthscope360^{TM}
- StrengthscopeTeam^{TM}
- Strengths Engagement Index^{TM}
- StrengthscopeLeader^{TM}.

Thinking strengths   This group of strengths concerns how you go about gathering and using information to make decisions.

Value   A value is a deeply held principle, belief or judgement that influences the way we think about ideas, behaviour, people or objects. Since we are emotionally attached to our values, they guide our day-to-day decisions and behaviour.

Zone of peak performance   The point where areas of competence (skills, knowledge and abilities) overlap with strengths (areas that energize us). It is in this area that we are most likely to be able to achieve peak performance.

Emotional Strengths

Courage: You take on challenges and face risks by standing up for what you believe

Emotional Control: You are aware of your emotional "triggers" and how to control these to remain calm and productive

Enthusiasm: You demonstrate passion and energy when communicating goals, beliefs, interests or ideas you feel strongly about

Optimism: You remain positive and upbeat about the future and your ability to influence it to your advantage

Resilience: You deal effectively with setbacks and enjoy overcoming difficult challenges

Self-confidence: You have a strong belief in yourself and your abilities to accomplish tasks and goals

Relational Strengths

Collaboration: You work cooperatively with others to overcome conflict and build towards a common goal

Compassion: You demonstrate a deep and genuine concern for the well-being of others

Developing Others: You promote other people's learning and development to help them achieve their goals and fulfil their potential

Empathy: You readily identify with other people's situations and can see things clearly from their perspective

Leading: You take responsibility for influencing and motivating others to contribute to the goals and success of their team and organization

Persuasiveness: You are able to win agreement and support for a position or desired outcome

Relationship Building: You take steps to build networks of contacts and act as a "hub" between people that you know

Thinking Strengths	Execution Strengths
Common Sense: You make pragmatic judgements based on practical thinking and previous experience	**Decisiveness:** You make quick, confident and clear decisions, even when faced with limited information
Creativity: You come up with new ideas and original solutions to move things forward	**Efficiency:** You take a well-ordered and methodical approach to tasks to achieve planned outcomes
Critical Thinking: You approach problems and arguments by breaking them down systematically and objectively evaluating them	**Flexibility:** You remain adaptable and flexible in the face of unfamiliar or changing situations
Detail Orientation: You pay attention to detail in order to produce high quality output, no matter what the pressures	**Initiative:** You take independent action to make things happen and achieve goals
Strategic Mindedness: You focus on the future and take a strategic perspective on issues and challenges	**Results Focus:** You maintain a strong sense of focus on results, driving tasks and projects to completion
	Self-improvement: You draw on a wide range of people and resources in the pursuit of self-development and learning

About the Authors

James Brook, Director, Strengths Partnership Ltd
James is co-founder and director of Strengths Partnership. He has over 20 years' experience in leadership development, innovative assessment, organizational change and talent management, having worked in consulting and corporate roles internationally. Recent clients have included Facebook, ING Direct, Novartis Pharmaceuticals, Photobox, Takeda Pharmaceuticals, GSK and Tesco.

James is a regular speaker on strengths-focused leadership and talent development and has contributed a wide range of business and professional publications in the area. He has a Master's Degree in Industrial and Organizational Psychology, an MBA and is a Fellow of the CIPD.

Dr Paul Brewerton, Director, Strengths Partnership Ltd
Paul is co-founder and director of Strengths Partnership. Paul is a Chartered Occupational Psychologist and holds a Doctorate in Organizational Psychology with around 20 years' experience in individual, team and organizational development. Paul has worked across a wide variety of sectors, recent clients include Takeda, Tesco, Legal and General, Panasonic, Santander, Asda, Royal Air Force, BNP Paribas and many more.

In recent years, Paul has dedicated his business activities to helping organizations translate a strengths-focused approach to bottom-line business performance. He is a frequent contributor to business publications and regular conference speaker.

Strengths Partnership Ltd

Strengths Partnership (www.strengthspartnership.com) is a global leader in business psychology and leadership development dedicated to helping organizations deliver positive workplaces and peak performance.

Our Strengthscope® system (www.strengthscope.com) is the world's most complete and innovative strengths profiling system that helps energize peak performance at work.

We have five consulting practice areas: Leadership Development, Organization Development, Team Development, Talent Assessment and Strengths Coaching.

Our values shape our culture and the way we work with clients. We strive to live our values of Passion, Pragmatism, Professionalism and Partnership everyday through our actions and decisions.